Reveal, Reduce, Succeed: Uncover Hidden Logistics Costs

LOGISTICS IN THE BLIND SPOT: FINDING THE COSTS YOU DON'T SEE

Logistics In The Blind Spot: Finding The Costs You Don't See is a strategic guide that unveils the hidden costs in third-party logistics and offers actionable solutions for identifying and eliminating them.

DWAYNE FARR

Logistics In The Blind Spot: Finding The Costs You Don't See

The Cost You Never Calculated

Let's Talk Dollars and Cents First

Alright, let's delve into the nitty-gritty of your business's financial landscape. We need to put on our detective hats and start scrutinizing where every dollar comes from and where it goes. It's time to dissect those expenses that often skulk in the shadows, evading detection like elusive phantoms. These sneaky costs can seriously throw your budget for a loop if you don't keep a close watch. From direct expenses like labor, transportation, and materials, to the not-so-obvious overhead costs and potential opportunity costs, we will peel back the layers of your financial operations. Take labor costs, for instance – it's not just about the hourly wages but also the associated payroll taxes, benefits, training, and maybe even overtime. Then there's the labyrinth of transportation expenses, such as fuel, maintenance, insurance, and unexpected hiccups along the supply chain. Each seemingly innocuous expense adds up, playing hide and seek with your profits. But wait, that's not all! Let's not forget the indirect costs that lurk in the shadows, whispering their influence on your bottom line. These could include the intangible impact of poor communication, missed opportunities due to inefficiencies, or the insidious effects of undetected errors and delays. Moreover, the hidden fees and surprises that suddenly rear their ugly heads without warning – an unexpected charge here, an unplanned-for expense there – can leave you reeling. All these cryptic costs muddy the waters and distort your true financial picture. So, isn't it high time we shine a bright light on these murky corners of your expenditure? By revealing and understanding these sorcerous expenses, we can navigate through the maze to uncover areas of potential savings and growth. Stay with me as we unravel this captivating detective story of dollars and cents.

Why Your Expenses Play Hide and Seek

Ever found yourself scratching your head at the end of the month, wondering where all your hard-earned dollars disappeared to? You meticulously budgeted for every major expense, tracked down those sneaky little discretionary costs, and yet, the bottom line doesn't seem to add up. It's like playing a game of hide and seek with your own finances. But here's the thing – it's not you, it's them. Your expenses have a knack for eluding detection. Let's delve into the reasons behind this perplexing phenomenon.

First off, the sheer volume of transactions in today's business world can make it feel like you're drowning in a sea of numbers. With money flowing in and out from various channels, keeping tabs on every cent becomes a Herculean task. Hidden fees, unexpected charges, and unaccounted-for expenditures lurk within the labyrinthine layers of financial data.

Furthermore, the complexity of modern business operations only serves to exacerbate this conundrum. From intricate supply chains to diverse service providers, the web of interconnected financial activities creates ample opportunities for expenses to slip through the cracks. Then there's the thorny issue of nuanced cost categorization – some expenses wear multiple hats, making it challenging to pin them down to a specific ledger entry.

Let's not forget the human factor. Miscommunication, oversight, or simply human error can inject ambiguity into your expenditure records. That supplier payment that got lost in the shuffle, the contract term that nobody remembered to revise – these are the little landmines that wreak havoc on your financial equilibrium. And when it comes to the fine print of financial agreements, deciphering the cryptic language of contracts might as well be translating ancient hieroglyphs.

Lastly, the ever-changing landscape of external factors makes it near impossible to predict and control all expenses. Inflation, market fluctuations, regulatory changes – the external environment is a wild card that can throw even the most meticulous budgets off-kilter. It's like chasing an elusive mirage; just when you think you've got a handle on your expenses, they slip away and morph into something unforeseen.

So, why do your expenses play hide and seek? It's not your lack of financial acumen; it's the intricate dance of factors in the modern business ecosystem. But fear not, understanding these elusive dynamics is the first step towards shedding light on your finances and uncovering the hidden treasures within.

The Other Side of the Coin – Unseen Efficiencies

Consider this: while you're busy crunching numbers and scrutinizing every expense line, there's a whole other realm of opportunities waiting to be unearthed. We tend to focus so much on costs that we often overlook the potential for hidden efficiencies. These are the unsung heroes that can transform your operations and ultimately impact your bottom line in ways you never imagined. Let's delve into the realm of unseen efficiencies and uncover how they hold the potential to reshape your entire approach. Picture this scenario: you've been investing significant resources in a particular process, thinking that it's the only way things can be done. But what if there's a more efficient method waiting to be discovered behind the curtain? It's crucial to shift our perspective from solely managing expenses to understanding the true value behind each action and the potential for streamlining operations. Unseen efficiencies could manifest in various forms – it might be reallocating resources to optimize workflow, leveraging technology to automate repetitive tasks, or even reimagining the supply chain to cut down on unnecessary steps. By honing in on these hidden gems, not only do you stand to cut unnecessary costs, but you also unlock the door to heightened productivity and agility. Embracing the concept of unseen efficiencies requires a shift in mindset. It's about challenging the status quo and being open to rethinking traditional approaches. This entails fostering a culture of continuous improvement, where everyone within the organization is encouraged to explore, question, and innovate. After all, the most groundbreaking solutions often emerge when we dare to look beyond the surface. Furthermore, identifying unseen efficiencies demands a keen eye for detail and a willingness to question every aspect of your current operations. Sometimes, the most significant gains stem from the smallest tweaks, and that level of scrutiny can only come from a commitment to uncovering every inefficiency. As we venture deeper into the realm of unseen efficiencies, remember that this isn't just about cutting costs; it's about laying the groundwork for sustainable growth and resilience. The journey may require dedicated resources and time, but the rewards are nothing short of transformative. So, let's step beyond the obvious and embrace the untapped potential that lies within the realm of unseen efficiencies.

Unpacking Overhead Costs Like a Pro

Let's delve into the labyrinth of overhead costs – those silent spenders that slyly nibble away at your bottom line. You might not even realize how much they're draining from your resources until you start to investigate them closely. These are the sneaky expenses that often lurk behind the scenes, masquerading as necessary evils or necessary investments. At first glance, they might seem insignificant, but once you start peeling back the layers, you'll uncover a whole web of interconnected expenses that can catch you off guard. From administrative and operational costs to utility bills and office supplies, these seemingly small outlays add up faster than you can say 'budget.' Managing overhead costs effectively means playing detective. It's about tracking every cent that leaves your coffers, pinpointing areas where costs could be trimmed, and seeking out more efficient alternatives. Don't be fooled by appearances – sometimes what seems essential may actually be obsolete or overpriced. Unpacking overhead costs involves a meticulous examination of every line item on your expense sheet, questioning if each cost is truly indispensable or if there's room for optimization. This process demands a critical eye, strategic thinking, and the willingness to shake up established routines if it means saving valuable dollars. Remember, the goal isn't just to cut costs at random but to allocate resources more judiciously, ensuring that every penny spent contributes directly to your overall efficiency and profitability. Furthermore, it's not just about singling out expenses; it's also about identifying opportunities for cost-saving measures. This could involve renegotiating contracts, exploring alternative suppliers, or implementing innovative strategies to streamline operations without compromising quality. By the time you're through unpacking your overhead costs like a pro, you'll emerge armed with a newfound sense of financial acumen and the confidence to make savvy decisions about your spending. No longer will these covert outlays stay hidden in the shadows, siphoning away your earnings. Instead, you'll have a clear understanding of where your money is going, and more importantly, how to rein it in effectively.

Opportunity Costs - The Invisible Competitor

When it comes to assessing your logistics operations, the visible costs are just the tip of the iceberg. Often overlooked and underestimated, opportunity costs represent the untold story within your business. These silent adversaries quietly chip away at your bottom line, manifesting as the price of missed opportunities, underutilized resources, and suboptimal decision-making. In today's fast-paced and dynamic marketplace, where every moment counts, failing to recognize and mitigate these opportunity costs can spell disaster for your competitive edge. Let's delve deeper into this hidden world of opportunity costs and explore how they rival even the most formidable of external competitors. Imagine a scenario where you allocate valuable resources to one aspect of your operations, only to later realize that another area was primed for exponential growth. This oversight not only represents a lost opportunity but also ties up vital assets in a less profitable venture, constraining your ability to adapt and thrive in an evolving landscape. Recognizing and quantifying these opportunity costs is akin to unmasking a shrewd adversary—you begin to comprehend the full impact of overlooked choices and latent potential. From delayed market entries and inefficient inventory management to the repercussions of misaligned partnerships, every decision carries its own set of opportunity costs. Furthermore, the insidious nature of opportunity costs lies in their pervasive influence; they lurk in every facet of your business, silently siphoning off potential gains and eroding your competitive advantage. It's like competing against an invisible adversary—one that exploits your oversight and thrives on the precious seconds, resources, and opportunities that slip through the cracks. Picture this: Every minute your team spends addressing a subpar process or navigating a convoluted supply chain, the true cost of lost time begins to mount. The opportunity cost of not streamlining your operations reverberates far beyond the immediate inefficiencies, stifling innovation and hindering your capacity to set industry benchmarks. So, what's the antidote to this hidden nemesis? It starts with fostering a culture of astute decision-making and ingrained awareness of the unseen costs lingering behind every choice. By embracing a holistic approach to cost assessment, you can uncover the intricacies of opportunity costs and strategically reallocate resources to capitalize on your full potential. Remember, in the labyrinthine realm of modern logistics, victory isn't just about outcompeting external forces—it's about mastering the art of mitigating opportunity costs and harnessing every overlooked possibility for sustained success.

When Bad Communication Becomes Costly

In the world of logistics, bad communication can be a silent killer—leaving a trail of missed deadlines, misunderstood expectations, and frustrated clients in its wake. Whether it's a misinterpreted email, confusing instructions, or delayed responses, poor communication within the 3PL ecosystem can quickly spiral into costly consequences. Consider a scenario where a vital shipment's urgency wasn't effectively communicated, leading to delivery delays and customer dissatisfaction. This not only impacts your bottom line but also tarnishes your brand reputation. Moreover, ineffective communication between you and your 3PL provider might result in inaccurate forecasting, which can lead to excess inventory, higher holding costs, and potential stockouts. The domino effect of these communication breakdowns can erode trust and strain partnerships. Without clear and timely communication, crucial updates regarding market conditions, inventory status, or changing customer demands may get lost in translation, leaving both parties vulnerable to unnecessary risks and financial losses. When there's a lack of transparency and open dialogue, it creates an environment ripe for errors, misunderstandings, and finger-pointing. These communication mishaps can trigger additional overheads as teams rush to rectify avoidable mistakes. Inefficiencies caused by poor communication manifest in various areas, including operational disruptions, escalations of conflict, and unanticipated expenses. To mitigate this, it's essential to foster a culture of effective communication, setting clear expectations, utilizing precise language, and establishing multiple communication channels for different scenarios. This ensures that critical information is conveyed accurately and efficiently, preventing costly misunderstandings and delays. By prioritizing open lines of communication with your 3PL partner, both parties can proactively address issues, align strategies, and adapt swiftly to market fluctuations. Investing in robust communication protocols upfront can ultimately save tremendous time, resources, and money in the long run, while fortifying the resilience of your supply chain.

Hidden Fees and Surprises You Never Signed Up For

Ever felt like your bills are playing hide-and-seek with your budget? It's often the case when it comes to working with third-party logistics providers. Sure, you sign on the dotted line for a certain fee or service, but what about the hidden charges that lurk beneath the surface? These sneaky surprises can quickly turn a seemingly lucrative deal into a financial nightmare.

Let's start with those unassuming extra fees that tend to pop up out of nowhere. From administrative charges and handling costs to storage fees and special request expenses, the list is never-ending. And guess what? They all conveniently seem to escape the spotlight during the initial negotiations. It's as if they're master illusionists, appearing only when the bill arrives.

But wait, there's more! Have you ever thought about the opportunity costs associated with working with a 3PL? Sure, they handle the logistics, but what about the business opportunities you missed while dealing with inefficiencies or delays caused by your provider's shortcomings? That's money slipping through your fingers without you even realizing it. A delayed shipment here, a mishandled order there – the ripple effect of these

small hiccups can end up costing you much more than you bargained for.
And don't get me started on the indirect costs that come knocking at your door uninvited. When processes aren't streamlined, and communication breaks down, it's not just your bottom line that suffers. Employee morale, customer satisfaction, and your brand reputation can take a hit too. Suddenly, that attractive deal you signed doesn't seem so appealing anymore.
These are the hard truths that many businesses learn the hard way. But fear not! By shedding light on these unseen expenses and potential pitfalls, you're equipped to make informed decisions and safeguard your resources. As we delve deeper, we'll uncover strategies to keep these surprise costs in check and ensure that what you signed up for is indeed what you get. Prepare to reclaim control over your expenditures and leave those pesky hidden fees in the rearview mirror.

The Ripple Effect – Indirect Costs You Didn't Expect

When it comes to evaluating the cost of third-party logistics (3PL), the focus often centers on the immediate expenses and charges. However, there's a whole world of indirect costs that tend to fly under the radar, only to make their presence known in unexpected ways. These indirect costs can emanate from various sources within the 3PL relationship, and understanding their impact requires a keen eye for detail. Let's delve into the intricate web of indirect costs present in your 3PL partnership.

One of the most prevalent indirect costs stems from inefficiencies in processes and operations. When these inefficiencies go unnoticed and unaddressed, they compound over time, resulting in lost productivity, wasted resources, and ultimately increased costs. Such inefficiencies could be anything from suboptimal inventory management to inefficient transportation routes, all of which have far-reaching consequences.

Moreover, the people problem, although previously discussed, also contributes significantly to indirect costs. Employee turnover, lack of training, or miscommunication can lead to errors, delays, and rework, amplifying the hidden costs embedded in the 3PL relationship. These seemingly small issues can manifest as ripple effects, affecting not just one area but the entirety of the supply chain in subtle yet impactful ways.

In today's interconnected world, technology and integration gaps are another major source of indirect costs. Inadequate systems or disjointed technological setups can result in compatibility issues, data discrepancies, and operational hiccups. The ripple effect of these tech-related problems may not be immediately visible, but it gradually translates into increased lead times, customer dissatisfaction, and ultimately financial repercussions.

Lastly, overlooked communication breakdowns between you and your 3PL partner can lead to indirect costs that permeate throughout the collaboration. Misunderstandings, lack of transparency, and ineffective problem-solving mechanisms can cause an array of interconnected issues, from order inaccuracies to missed opportunities for efficiency improvements. A breakdown in communication has a cascading effect, impacting multiple facets of the business and resulting in unforeseen costs.

Understanding and quantifying these indirect costs is pivotal in obtaining a holistic view of the true expense of your 3PL partnership. Often disguised as minor blips on the operational radar, these indirect costs can collectively evolve into substantial financial drawbacks. By recognizing and addressing these hidden expenses, you can set the stage for optimizing your 3PL relationship and mitigating the ripple effect of unforeseen costs.

Crunching the Numbers: ROI or Money Pit?

You've heard the saying 'knowledge is power,' and when it comes to understanding the true costs of your 3PL relationship, this phrase couldn't ring truer. Crunching the numbers to evaluate your return on investment (ROI) might seem like a daunting task, but it's an essential part of making informed decisions moving forward. Let's dive into the nitty-gritty of calculating the value you derive from your 3PL partnership. First, take a comprehensive look at all aspects of your logistics operations where the 3PL is involved. This includes not only direct financial costs but also the less tangible impacts on your business, such as customer satisfaction, delivery speed, and inventory management. It's crucial to consider both quantitative and qualitative factors when evaluating the true cost. A thorough analysis will help you uncover hidden expenses, identify areas for improvement, and assess the overall impact on your bottom line. Look beyond the surface level to unveil any inefficiencies or missed opportunities that may be costing your business dearly. Next, compare these findings against your initial expectations and objectives when engaging with a 3PL provider. Are you reaping the benefits you anticipated, or have unforeseen costs outweighed the perceived advantages? Understanding the complete picture enables you to distinguish between a worthwhile investment and a potential money pit. Furthermore, consider the opportunity cost of sticking with a subpar 3PL partnership. What growth avenues have been stifled, and how has this affected your competitiveness in the market? By identifying the resources, time, and potential revenue that could have been redirected elsewhere, you'll gain insights into the broader impacts of your decision. Remember to factor in not just immediate gains or losses but also long-term implications. Your 3PL's performance and contribution to your operational efficiency play significant roles in determining the true value they bring to your business. Finally, once you've crunched the numbers and evaluated the complete spectrum of costs and benefits associated with your 3PL, you'll gain a clearer understanding of whether it's truly delivering the value you need. Armed with this knowledge, you're better equipped to make strategic decisions that align with your business goals and drive sustainable growth.

No More Blind Spots - Calculating True Cost

When it comes to evaluating the true cost of your operations, it's crucial to consider every aspect of your business. The term 'true cost' encompasses far more than just the bottom line or the expenses that show up on a balance sheet. To truly understand the impact of your logistics operations on your business, you need to factor in not only the direct costs, but also the indirect ones that may be lurking in the shadows. Let's take a closer look at how to uncover and calculate the true cost of your logistics operations. First off, it's essential to scrutinize every component of your 3PL relationship, from the initial onboarding process to ongoing communication and performance evaluations. This involves delving into the specifics of your service level agreements, understanding the pricing models employed, and identifying any hidden fees or surprise expenses. Beyond these obvious financial considerations, it's equally important to analyze the impact of inefficient processes, technology gaps, and potential opportunity costs that could be affecting your bottom line. Often, the true cost of a 3PL relationship is obscured by inefficiencies in operations, lack of visibility, and poor communication. These factors can lead to missed opportunities, customer dissatisfaction, and ultimately, financial losses. It's also vital to assess the indirect costs associated with these shortcomings, such as the strain they may place on your internal resources and the potential for damaging your brand reputation. Moreover, failing to address performance issues within your 3PL relationship can result in lost time and effort spent on damage control and operational firefighting. By shining a light on these previously hidden costs, you can accurately evaluate the value your 3PL partnership brings to your business and identify areas for improvement. Furthermore, embracing transparency in your 3PL relationship means fostering open communication, setting clear expectations, and establishing mechanisms for ongoing performance measurement and evaluation. By consistently measuring and monitoring the true cost of your logistics operations, you can make informed decisions and drive efficiencies that positively impact your overall business performance. In doing so, you transition from a reactive stance to a proactive one, enabling your company to turn potential blind spots into strategic advantages. Ultimately, by calculating the true cost of your logistics operations, you empower your business to optimize its operations, improve customer satisfaction, and strengthen its competitive position within the marketplace.

Logistics In The Blind Spot: Finding The Costs You Don't See

What Is 3PL — and What It's Supposed to Do

Let's Talk 3PL: Unpacking the Basics

Today, let's delve into the fascinating world of 3PL—third-party logistics. It's like having a trusted ally who takes care of all the nitty-gritty details of your logistics and supply chain needs, allowing you to focus on your core business activities. Imagine a time when businesses were burdened with every aspect of their logistics operations. Then along came the concept of 3PL, offering a lifeline to streamline and optimize distribution, warehousing, transportation, and more. This modern approach to logistics management has its roots in the evolving needs of businesses to become leaner, more efficient, and globally competitive. By partnering with 3PL providers, companies have been able to tap into specialist expertise and resources to navigate the complexities of modern supply chains. The rise of 3PL is a testament to the dynamic nature of industry, where collaboration and specialization have emerged as crucial factors for success. As we venture further into our exploration of 3PL, we'll uncover the intricacies of this essential element in the contemporary business landscape.

A Walk Down Memory Lane: How 3PL Came to Be

Picture this: It's the mid-20th century, and supply chains are evolving at an unprecedented pace. Traditional businesses are grappling with the logistical challenges of a newly globalized marketplace. Out of this cacophony of change emerged the concept of third-party logistics (3PL) - a paradigm shift that would forever transform the way goods were moved, stored, and managed.

To understand how 3PL came to be, we need to turn back the clock to a time when businesses were waking up to the realization that they couldn't do it all on their own. Roll back to the era when companies began acknowledging that handling every aspect of their supply chain in-house was no longer sustainable or cost-effective.

Enter the first whispers of 3PL - a radical suggestion that companies could outsource elements of their logistics operations to specialized experts. This seismic shift allowed businesses to focus on their core competencies, while leaving the intricacies of transportation, warehousing, and fulfillment to those with the infrastructure and expertise to handle them.

Fast forward through the decades, and the 3PL industry has evolved in lockstep with advancements in technology, globalization, and consumer expectations. What began as a novel solution to complex logistical puzzles has blossomed into an indispensable component of modern supply chains.

As we traverse this chronological journey, we'll encounter trailblazing innovators who laid the groundwork for the 3PL landscape we know today. We'll uncover stories of resilience, adaptability, and the persistent pursuit of efficiency that propelled 3PL from a rudimentary concept to an intricate web of interconnected services.

By immersing ourselves in this historical narrative, we gain a profound appreciation for the evolution of 3PL, and the pivotal role it plays in shaping the contemporary business ecosystem. So, grab your metaphorical time machine as we embark on this enlightening expedition through the annals of logistics history.

The ABCs of 3PL Services: What's on Offer?

When it comes to 3PL services, the offerings can be quite diverse and comprehensive. At its core, third-party logistics (3PL) providers aim to seamlessly integrate and manage a range of supply chain functions for businesses, ensuring efficient and cost-effective operations. These services can encompass a wide array of activities, including transportation, warehousing, distribution, inventory management, freight forwarding, order fulfillment, and much more. 3PL providers can also offer value-added services such as packaging, labeling, kitting, and assembly to further streamline the supply chain. At the heart of 3PL services is the commitment to optimizing processes and enhancing the overall efficiency of logistics operations for businesses. 3PLs excel in leveraging their expertise and resources to handle complex logistics challenges that may be beyond the scope of in-house capabilities. By outsourcing these critical functions to 3PL providers, businesses can focus on their core competencies and strategic initiatives while benefitting from the specialized knowledge and economies of scale that 3PLs bring to the table. Additionally, 3PLs often have established networks, technology infrastructure, and industry insights that enable them to offer customized solutions tailored to the unique requirements of each client. This adaptability is particularly invaluable in today's dynamic and rapidly evolving business landscape. From managing global supply chains and navigating regulatory complexities to implementing innovative technologies and mitigating supply chain risks, 3PLs are equipped to tackle a myriad of logistical tasks with precision and agility. Furthermore, the breadth of 3PL services facilitates scalability, allowing businesses to adjust their logistics support as per fluctuating demands and market conditions without bearing the burden of fixed overhead costs. Overall, the comprehensive suite of 3PL services empowers businesses to drive operational excellence, enhance customer satisfaction, and gain a competitive edge in the marketplace.

Who's Who in the 3PL World

When delving into the world of third-party logistics (3PL), it's essential to understand the key players that make this complex ecosystem function seamlessly. At the heart of it all are the 3PL providers themselves. These entities come in various shapes and sizes, ranging from global giants with extensive networks to smaller, specialized firms catering to niche markets. Each brings its unique strengths and capabilities to the table, and understanding their differences is crucial for any business seeking 3PL services.

Beyond the providers, freight forwarders, carriers, and brokers also play integral roles in the 3PL landscape. Freight forwarders act as intermediaries between shippers and carriers, coordinating the movement of goods across different modes of transportation and international borders. Carriers, on the other hand, are responsible for physically transporting the cargo, whether by road, rail, air, or sea. Brokers facilitate the matchmaking of available carriers with shippers in need of transportation services, often adding value through their industry expertise and network connections.

Additionally, technology solutions providers have become indispensable contributors to modern 3PL operations. Their innovative software platforms and digital tools enable efficient management of supply chain processes, real-time tracking of shipments, and data-driven decision-making. In an era driven by technological advancements, these tech partners are instrumental in enhancing the overall capabilities and competitiveness of 3PL providers.

Furthermore, we cannot overlook the critical role played by regulatory bodies, industry associations, and trade organizations in shaping the 3PL landscape. They establish and enforce standards, provide guidance on best practices, and advocate for the interests of both service providers and their clients. By engaging with these entities, businesses can stay abreast of regulatory changes, industry trends, and emerging opportunities, enabling them to make informed decisions and navigate the evolving complexities of the 3PL environment.

Ultimately, comprehending the ecosystem of 3PL goes beyond recognizing these individual players—it involves understanding how they all intersect and collaborate to deliver value to businesses worldwide. As we continue our exploration of the 3PL realm, we'll unveil more layers of this interconnected web, shedding light on the collective impact of these key stakeholders and their contributions to the global supply chain.

More Than Just Boxes: The Role of 3PL

When people think about the role of a 3PL, their mind often jumps straight to the physical act of moving things from Point A to Point B. And it's true, that's definitely a big part of what they do. But there's so much more to it than just trucks and warehouses. In fact, the role of a 3PL is more like that of an orchestrator, carefully conducting a complex symphony of logistics, technology, and manpower. Picture this: You have multiple suppliers with different schedules and deadlines, various transportation options, customs regulations to navigate, and a multitude of ways your goods can be stored and delivered. It's a logistical puzzle that requires expertise and finesse to solve. This is where the 3PL comes in, putting all the pieces together while ensuring efficiency, cost-effectiveness, and timely delivery. They seamlessly coordinate all these moving parts, managing the entire supply chain with precision and agility. Beyond the coordination, 3PLs offer invaluable insights and analytics that help optimize not just your transportation and warehousing, but your entire operation. They bring visibility into your supply chain, allowing you to make informed decisions and adjustments as needed. It's not just about moving products; it's about leveraging data and experience to improve the overall performance of your business. Moreover, the role of a 3PL extends even further when they integrate technology and automation into the equation. They streamline processes, minimize errors, and enhance productivity through innovative solutions. Their ability to adapt and evolve with the ever-changing landscape of logistics is what sets them apart as crucial partners in modern business. In essence, 3PLs are catalysts for seamless supply chain operations, serving as the backbone that supports the smooth flow of products from origin to destination. Recognizing the depth and breadth of their role is essential for businesses seeking to maximize their operational efficiency and stay ahead in the competitive market.

Game Changer or Necessary Evil?

When it comes to third-party logistics (3PL), opinions can be quite polarized. Some view 3PL providers as a game changer — a strategic partner that offers invaluable expertise, resources, and capabilities. On the other hand, there are those who see 3PL as a necessary evil, a cost to be endured rather than an opportunity to be embraced. So, which viewpoint holds sway? Let's unpack this debate. It's undeniable that 3PL has the potential to be a game changer for businesses of all sizes. By leveraging the specialized knowledge and infrastructure of a 3PL provider, companies can streamline their operations, expand their reach, and enhance their overall efficiency. For many businesses, partnering with a nimble and innovative 3PL provider has paved the way for growth and success. However, there's also the camp that views 3PL as a necessary evil, perhaps due to past experiences or lingering misconceptions. They may see 3PL as a potential source of added complexity, cost, or even loss of control over key aspects of their supply chain. These concerns are not unfounded, as not every 3PL partnership delivers on its promises. Poor communication, unclear expectations, or mismatched priorities can sometimes turn a 3PL relationship into more of an ordeal than an opportunity. The truth, as is often the case, lies somewhere in between. Yes, 3PL can be a game changer, but it demands careful vetting and clear alignment of goals to truly realize its potential. This involves addressing fears head-on, clarifying expectations, and establishing transparent and open lines of communication. Balancing the scales between game changer and necessary evil comes down to finding the right 3PL partner and cultivating a collaborative, mutually beneficial relationship. When these elements align, the benefits can undoubtedly outweigh the challenges. So, whether you currently view 3PL as a game changer, a necessary evil, or something in between, it's essential to recognize that the dynamics of the relationship can be shaped and steered. As we navigate through the complexities and opportunities presented by 3PL, let's remember that the outcome is ultimately determined by how both parties approach and interact within this critical partnership.

How 3PLs Blend Art with Science

When it comes to third-party logistics (3PL), one might assume that it's all about cold, hard data, numbers, and efficiency. And while these elements are undoubtedly crucial, there's a whole other side to the story that often goes unnoticed—the art of logistics. Believe it or not, successful 3PL providers don't just crunch numbers and streamline processes; they also integrate creativity, intuition, and adaptability into their approach. This harmonious blend of art and science is what sets exceptional 3PLs apart from the rest. Let's delve into how this fusion takes place.

Firstly, let's consider the science of logistics. This involves leveraging advanced technologies, data analytics, and predictive modeling to optimize supply chain operations. From forecasting demand and managing inventory levels to route optimization and warehouse automation, the scientific aspect of 3PL is about harnessing innovation to drive efficiency and cost savings. Yet, without the human touch, even the most sophisticated algorithms can't fully grasp the nuances of real-world logistics challenges. This leads us to the art of logistics—where experience, intuition, and adaptability become the guiding forces behind smart decision-making.

The artful component of 3PL involves understanding the unique dynamics of each client's business, empathizing with their pain points, and tailoring solutions that go beyond mere numerical optimization. Seasoned 3PL professionals rely on their deep industry knowledge, honed over years of hands-on experience, to navigate complex scenarios and facilitate seamless operations. Fostering strong relationships with clients, suppliers, and carriers is another facet of the 'art'—it's about communication, collaboration, and trust, which can't be quantified on a spreadsheet.

Moreover, the art of logistics encompasses adaptability—the ability to pivot swiftly and innovate in response to unforeseen disruptions or changing market dynamics. Unlike the rigidity of pure science, the art factor allows 3PLs to improvise, think outside the box, and craft bespoke solutions that align with the client's unique business goals. This flexibility often proves to be the differentiating factor in delivering exceptional value amidst turbulent times.

Ultimately, the magic of exceptional 3PL lies in striking the perfect balance between the rigor of science and the finesse of art. It's about understanding that while data and technology provide the backbone, it's the human ingenuity, empathy, and adaptability that breathe life into every logistical solution. When 3PL providers seamlessly blend the logical with the intuitive, the results speak for themselves—greater resilience, agility, and transformative impact on the businesses they serve.

Let's Bust Some Myths About 3PL

When it comes to third-party logistics (3PL), there's no shortage of myths and misconceptions floating around. Let's shine a light on some of these false beliefs and set the record straight. One common myth is that hiring a 3PL provider means relinquishing control. In reality, a good 3PL partnership is all about collaboration, transparency, and synergy. It's not about giving up control; it's about gaining a strategic partner who can enhance your operations.

Another widespread misconception is that 3PLs are a one-size-fits-all solution. This couldn't be further from the truth. Effective 3PL providers understand that each client has unique needs and challenges, and they tailor their services accordingly. From customized inventory management to personalized supply chain solutions, a reputable 3PL goes above and beyond cookie-cutter approaches.

There's also the misconception that 3PLs only add cost without delivering substantial value. This couldn't be farther from reality. The right 3PL partner can unlock hidden efficiencies, streamline processes, and optimize your supply chain in ways that directly impact your bottom line. A well-aligned 3PL relationship should result in cost savings, improved service levels, and enhanced scalability.

Some believe that integrating a 3PL into their operations will create more headaches than solutions. However, with advanced technology and robust integration capabilities, modern 3PLs seamlessly merge with their clients' systems, leading to streamlined workflows and real-time visibility.

Furthermore, a prevalent myth surrounding 3PLs is that they only focus on large enterprises and neglect smaller businesses. In truth, many 3PL providers specialize in catering to the specific needs of small and medium-sized businesses, offering scalable solutions that align with their unique requirements and growth trajectories.

Lastly, some may view 3PLs as mere transactional service providers rather than strategic partners. The reality is that a well-matched 3PL should act as an extension of your team, providing insights, expertise, and guidance that extend far beyond the scope of traditional logistics services.

By dispelling these myths, we can pave the way for businesses to embrace the transformative potential of 3PL partnerships, driving efficiency, innovation, and growth.

What a Good 3PL Should Really Do for You

When you've entrusted the logistics of your business to a third-party provider, you rightly expect them to deliver more than just moving boxes from one point to another. A good 3PL should be a true partner in your success, operating as an extension of your brand and striving to enhance your supply chain operations in meaningful ways.

First and foremost, a reliable 3PL should offer transparency and communication at every step of the process. You should never feel left in the dark about the status of your shipments or the performance of your logistics network. Whether it's real-time visibility through advanced tracking systems or proactive updates on potential disruptions, clear and constant communication is non-negotiable.

Beyond this, a good 3PL should provide tailored solutions that truly align with your unique business needs. This means going beyond cookie-cutter services and offering customized strategies that optimize efficiency, reduce costs, and mitigate risks specific to your industry and operations.

In addition to these core responsibilities, a standout 3PL goes the extra mile by leveraging technology and data-driven insights to streamline processes and drive continuous improvement. From leveraging AI and automation to harnessing predictive analytics for demand forecasting, a proactive 3PL is constantly scanning the horizon for opportunities to enhance your bottom line.

Lastly, but certainly not least, a good 3PL radiates reliability and adaptability. They should not only uphold high standards in meeting service-level agreements and compliance requirements but also demonstrate agility in responding to unexpected challenges and market shifts. Your 3PL shouldn't just meet expectations – they should exceed them, becoming an indispensable asset in navigating the complexities of modern supply chain management.

In the next chapter, we'll delve into preparing for the future challenges that lie ahead, equipping you with the knowledge and insight to ensure that your 3PL partnership evolves in sync with your business aspirations.

Looking Ahead: Setting Up for the Next Challenges

As we navigate the dynamic landscape of logistics and supply chain management, it's critical to anticipate the ever-evolving challenges that lie ahead. Whether it's the increasing demand for faster delivery times or the growing emphasis on sustainability, adapting to these changes is essential for success. Embracing technology will undoubtedly play a pivotal role in addressing these challenges. From advanced analytics to robotics and automated warehousing, staying ahead of the curve will require strategic investments in cutting-edge solutions.

Moreover, fostering strong partnerships with 3PL providers will be crucial in preparing for what's to come. Collaborating closely with your 3PL to align on goals, performance metrics, and risk mitigation strategies can help fortify your supply chain against future disruptions. It's all about building resilience and agility into the framework of your logistics operations.

Looking ahead also entails a deep dive into regulatory compliance and international trade dynamics. With an increasingly complex global marketplace, understanding the intricacies of cross-border regulations and tariffs becomes paramount. Organizations must proactively position themselves to navigate geopolitical shifts, trade policies, and potential trade wars to ensure minimal impact on their supply chains.

Furthermore, the rise of e-commerce and omnichannel distribution presents both opportunities and obstacles. Understanding consumer behavior, last-mile delivery challenges, and the need for seamless order fulfillment will be essential in shaping the future of logistics. By strategically positioning your logistics network to cater to evolving consumer preferences, you can stay ahead of the curve and maintain a competitive edge.

Amidst these impending challenges, environmental sustainability emerges as a non-negotiable imperative. The push for eco-friendly practices and reducing carbon footprints necessitates a reevaluation of traditional supply chain models. Initiatives such as sustainable packaging, alternative transportation methods, and energy-efficient warehouse operations are becoming integral components of the logistical landscape.

In conclusion, the road ahead is paved with uncertainties and complexities, demanding proactive adaptation and innovative solutions. By leveraging technological advancements, strengthening partnerships, navigating regulatory landscapes, understanding consumer dynamics, and embracing sustainability, businesses can lay a robust foundation to thrive amid the evolving challenges of the logistics and supply chain ecosystem.

Logistics In The Blind Spot: Finding The Costs You Don't See

Where the Blind Spots Begin

Setting the Scene: The Silence Before the Storm

You've probably heard the phrase 'the silence before the storm.' It's that eerie calm just before chaos descends, an unsettling hush that hints at the impending turbulence. In the world of 3PL engagements, this silence can be deceptive. As you embark on a new partnership with a third-party logistics provider, it's easy to get caught up in the excitement of potential cost savings, streamlined operations, and expanded capabilities. However, amidst this sense of anticipation, there are often subtle cues that go unnoticed, indicators of potential blind spots and challenges lurking on the horizon. These early stages of the relationship are critical, as they set the tone for what follows. It's during this lull that the first inklings of misalignment or overlooked details may appear. Yet, these warning signs can be deceptively quiet, easily dismissed or overlooked in the eagerness to get started. Often, it's only in retrospect that we recognize these early signals as the tiny ripples that precede significant disruptions. This section aims to shine a light on these less obvious markers, urging you to pay close attention to the nuances, the unsaid, and the unexplored. We'll explore how seemingly small misalignments can snowball into larger issues and how the seeds of future challenges may be sown in these initial moments of collaboration. By honing in on these subtleties, you can better prepare for the storm that may lie ahead, navigating the early stages of your 3PL partnership with eyes wide open.

What You Don't Know Can Cost You

Unseen corners and hidden costs plague even the most carefully managed supply chains. The truth is, what you don't know can cost you dearly. It's not just about the visible expenditures; it's the insidious undercurrents that ripple through your operations, quietly siphoning off resources and eroding your bottom line. Picture this: a warehouse teeming with goods, but an invisible inefficiency slowing down every step of the process. The cost? Not just in dollars but in customer satisfaction and missed opportunities. When you're in the dark about the inner workings of your 3PL relationship, you're essentially flying blind. Imagine the impact on your business when delays, errors, or miscommunications go undetected until it's too late. Every hiccup, bottleneck, or untracked movement incurs a toll, yet without insight into these blind spots, your company continues to bleed resources. While the numbers might stay hidden, the consequences are all too real. These unseen costs chip away at your competitive edge, hobbling your agility and clouding your decision-making. What's at stake isn't just profit margins; it's your ability to adapt and thrive in a dynamic marketplace. The price of ignorance extends beyond the financial realm, seeping into the very fabric of your company's reputation and long-term viability. As we delve into this crucial aspect, be prepared to uncover the startling dimensions of unawareness. By shedding light on the concealed expenses lurking within your 3PL operations, we aim to equip you with the knowledge and insights necessary to prevent these unseen costs from running rampant. Knowledge truly is power, and the first step in reclaiming control begins with acknowledging the potential impact of what's tragically overlooked.

Unseen Corners and Hidden Costs

In the world of logistics, the path to efficiency is paved with countless hidden corners, each concealing potential pitfalls and unexpected expenses. These unseen areas create a breeding ground for inefficiencies and costs that, if left unchecked, can wreak havoc on your bottom line. It's not just about what's visible on the surface; it's about delving into the shadows and shedding light on the nooks and crannies that are often overlooked. When we talk about hidden costs, we're not just referring to the obvious expenses such as transportation and storage. We're talking about the less apparent yet equally impactful drains on your resources. Think about it: the time spent manually inputting data, the rework caused by miscommunication, the delays resulting from poor coordination—all these factors contribute to the grand web of hidden costs. The complexity conundrum only amplifies these challenges. Multiple layers of processes and systems intertwine, creating a tangled web of intricacy that obscures the true extent of these hidden costs. It's like navigating through a maze blindfolded; you might eventually reach your destination, but you'll encounter numerous setbacks along the way. What exacerbates this issue is the lack of visibility – the inability to see through these layers to identify where the real problems lie. The complexity of the supply chain management landscape demands a keen eye and a deep understanding of its inner workings. Yet, all too often, these complexities act as a smokescreen, shrouding the true nature of the challenges at hand. As a result, organizations find themselves grappling with unforeseen expenses and operational inefficiencies that slowly eat away at their profitability. It's crucial to shine a light into these obscure corners and bring to surface the subtle yet impactful costs that lurk within. By doing so, you can begin to peel back the layers of complexity, revealing the underlying issues and devising strategic solutions to untangle the web of hidden costs. So, let's embark on an illuminating journey through these unseen corners, uncovering the hidden costs that lie in wait, and arming ourselves with the knowledge needed to navigate the labyrinth of logistics with clarity and confidence.

The Complexity Conundrum

Ever feel like you're lost in a labyrinth of logistics? Welcome to the complexity conundrum. As businesses grow and evolve, so does the intricacy of their supply chain operations. The maze of interconnected processes, partners, and technologies can quickly spiral into a headache-inducing tangle that seems impossible to unravel. It's like trying to solve a Rubik's Cube blindfolded. You twist and turn, hoping for a breakthrough, but often end up back where you started. The more you delve into it, the more layers of complexity reveal themselves. Each layer brings with it a new set of challenges, from compliance issues to capacity constraints. And just when you think you've got it all figured out, a new variable enters the equation, throwing everything off balance. Take a deep breath, because you're not alone. Many businesses grapple with the complexity conundrum, struggling to find clarity amidst the chaos. This section will delve into the heart of the conundrum, dissecting its various components and shedding light on strategies to navigate through the labyrinth. We'll explore the intricacies of multi-modal transportation, inventory management, and demand forecasting, each adding its own layer of complexity to the puzzle. But fear not, we won't leave you hanging in the labyrinth. Instead, we'll equip you with tools to untangle the web of complexities and turn them into opportunities for efficiency and growth. So grab your compass and join us as we embark on a journey through the complexity conundrum.

Communication Gaps: A Chasm We Overlook

Communication, they say, is the key to any successful relationship. Instead, when it comes to the complex dance between shippers and 3PL providers, communication gaps often emerge as the chasm that we overlook. It's all too easy for information to get lost in translation, for assumptions to go unchallenged, and for expectations to remain unvoiced. This chapter exposes the myriad ways in which these gaps can widen and deepen, impacting every aspect of the partnership. The first layer of this chasm often forms at the very outset, as mismatched expectations about communication frequency and transparency take root. Shippers may presume a certain level of real-time updates and visibility, only to find out that their 3PL provider operates on a different wavelength. Similarly, providers may assume that certain issues are not a priority for the shipper, leading to crucial details falling through the cracks. As operations unfold, the communication gap can manifest in divergent interpretations of performance metrics and KPIs. Both parties might be looking at the same data, yet drawing entirely different conclusions. This discord can snowball into disjointed strategies and missed opportunities for improvement. Beyond the quantitative realm, miscommunication can sow seeds of mistrust and frustration in the personal interactions between stakeholders. From micromanagement tendencies to an absence of constructive feedback, the human element becomes a casualty of unchecked communication gaps. Overlaying these challenges is the technological layer, where incompatible systems and inadequate integration only serve to widen the communication chasm. Siloed data sources and disjointed platforms impede the flow of critical information, exacerbating the already precarious situation. The toll of these communication gaps reverberates throughout the supply chain, casting a shadow over efficiency, productivity, and ultimately, profitability. But fear not, for recognizing the extent of and causes behind these communication gaps is the first step toward bridging the chasm. In the following section, we will delve into how rebuilding trust and syncing communication channels can help span the gulf that threatens to undermine the entire partnership.

The Trust Fall Without a Safety Net

In the world of logistics and supply chain management, trust is often considered the glue that holds everything together. It's the unspoken understanding between businesses and their 3PL partners, the belief that each party is fully committed to the success of the other. But what happens when that trust is put to the test? Picture this: you're relying on your 3PL partner to handle a crucial shipment for a major client. You've provided all the necessary information, gone over the details, and sent the goods on their way, confident that your partner will deliver as promised. But as hours turn into days, you start to feel the uneasy weight of uncertainty settling in. Where is your shipment? Why haven't you received any updates? The trust that was once so solid begins to crack under the pressure of unanswered questions. This is the trust fall without a safety net. When communication falters and transparency is lacking, trust becomes fragile. It's like standing on the edge of a cliff, hoping that your partner will catch you if you fall, only to realize that they were never prepared to be your safety net. In the absence of a safety net, doubts creep in, and the foundation of trust begins to crumble. Instead of feeling supported, you find yourself teetering on the edge, questioning every decision and second-guessing every reliance you've placed on your 3PL partner. The consequences of this breakdown in trust can be significant. Delays, miscommunications, and errors can result in financial losses, damaged relationships, and tarnished reputations. So, how do we build a safety net for trust in the world of logistics and supply chain management? It starts with open and honest communication. Both parties must be willing to share information, ask questions, and address concerns transparently. Trust is nurtured through consistent and reliable exchanges, where each side feels heard and understood. Establishing clear expectations and accountability also goes a long way in creating a safety net for trust. When everyone knows what is expected of them and takes ownership of their responsibilities, the likelihood of misunderstandings and disappointments diminishes. Collaborative problem-solving and proactive issue resolution further reinforce the safety net of trust. By openly acknowledging challenges and working together to find solutions, both businesses and their 3PL partners can demonstrate their commitment to overcoming obstacles and preserving trust. As the saying goes, trust takes years to build, seconds to break, and forever to repair. In the realm of logistics and supply chain management, nurturing and safeguarding trust is not just a good practice – it's an essential lifeline that ensures the seamless flow of operations and sustained success. The trust fall without a safety net serves as a poignant reminder of the critical role trust plays in every aspect of the partnership between businesses and their 3PL providers.

Data, Data Everywhere but Not a Drop to Sync

Data, data everywhere, but not a drop to sync. You've probably felt this frustration more times than you care to admit. In the world of 3PL logistics, the challenge of managing and utilizing data is akin to trying to solve a jigsaw puzzle with missing pieces—it's maddening, to say the least. Picture this: you have an abundance of data pouring in from various sources—your 3PL provider, your internal systems, shippers, carriers, and more. But when it comes to syncing all this data into a coherent, actionable stream of information, that's where the real uphill battle begins. It's like having a thick fog descend before you, obscuring any meaningful insight or clarity. The root cause? Often, it's a lack of unified systems, inconsistent data formats, and an absence of standardized processes for data collection and synchronization. What should be a symphony of orchestrated data often ends up sounding more like a cacophony of discordant notes. This clash of information silos can lead to critical blind spots and missed opportunities. Imagine crucial performance metrics slipping through the cracks, delays in decision-making due to conflicting reports, and the overarching struggle to glean accurate insights from a sea of fragmented data. Your operational efficiency is at stake, and the consequences are far-reaching. The impact touches everything from customer satisfaction to cost management. So how can we resolve this data dilemma? First, let's acknowledge that data management isn't just about collecting numbers and figures; it's about enabling informed action. We need to shift the focus from mere data accumulation to robust data integration and harmonization. Imagine a scenario where data flows seamlessly across systems, speaking the same language and painting a clear picture of your logistics operations. This calls for investment in technology that facilitates data interoperability and standardization. But technology alone isn't the panacea. A collaborative effort between 3PL providers, your team, and other stakeholders is crucial to ensure that data synchronization becomes a priority. Clarity emerges when everyone speaks the same data-driven language. Furthermore, a keen eye on data quality is imperative. Not all data is created equal, and effective data governance is essential to discern the diamonds from the rough. By establishing clear protocols for data input, validation, and maintenance, you pave the way for a trustworthy and reliable data landscape. When data becomes a trusted ally rather than a formidable adversary, the shadows of uncertainty recede, and strategic decisions become clearer. As you embark on this journey toward synchronized data harmony, remember that the destination isn't just seamless data flow. Ultimately, it's about leveraging this synchronized data to fuel proactive decision-making and gain a competitive edge. When data syncs, strategies align, efficiencies thrive, and blind spots fade into the rearview mirror.

Common Missteps and Overlooked Details

Let's take a moment to delve into those common missteps and overlooked details that can often spell the difference between smooth operations and unforeseen chaos within the realm of 3PL partnerships. One of the most prevalent issues arises from the failure to conduct thorough due diligence when selecting a 3PL partner. This mistake could lead to a misalignment of values, goals, or capabilities, setting the stage for future strife. Aligning closely with this is the oversight of failing to outline and agree upon key performance indicators (KPIs) from the outset. Without clearly defined metrics, determining success or failure becomes a subjective endeavor, opening the door to disappointment and disputes. Some may disregard the vital step of scrutinizing the service agreement, presuming boilerplate contracts to be sufficient. However, overlooking the nitty-gritty specifics can result in unexpected costs, service level discrepancies, or unaddressed contingencies. The failure to establish robust lines of communication also ranks among the most prevalent mistakes. Effective communication serves as the backbone of any successful partnership, yet its significance is often underestimated. Moreover, underestimating the intricacies of technology and integration can cause entire systems to fall out of sync, leading to inefficiencies and errors. All too frequently, companies overlook the importance of proactive monitoring and continuous improvement, assuming that once the partnership is established, their job is done. This shortsightedness can lead to missed opportunities for optimization and innovation. These unnoticed details and neglectful steps may seem inconsequential at the outset, but they hold the potential to unravel even the most promising 3PL partnerships. It's imperative to recognize their impact and proactively address them through meticulous attention to detail and unwavering commitment.

Reflecting on Real-Life Tangles

Real-life tangles are the knots in our businesses that, at first glance, seem too tight to undo. These are the stories whispered over office cubicles, the frustrating moments dissected during Monday morning meetings, and the hurdles that often feel insurmountable. Reflecting on these tangles is like tracing a tangled web with our fingertips - the more we explore, the more we uncover. Take for example a distribution challenge that seemed straightforward until it wasn't, or a miscommunication that led to a series of costly errors. These real-life scenarios can test our patience, force us to pivot, and demand our full attention. As we reflect on these tangles, we realize how interconnected each decision, process, and relationship truly is. We see that even the smallest oversight can trigger a chain reaction that ricochets through our entire operation. These tangles remind us of the intricacies of our business landscape, urging us to approach every detail with care and thoroughness. This section is about acknowledging these tangles not as barriers, but as opportunities for learning and growth. It's a dive into the messy, chaotic side of business that often goes unspoken. By confronting and learning from these tangles, we gain insights that shape our strategies, fortify our relationships, and prepare us for the unexpected. Together, let's navigate through these real-life tangles, unraveling their complexities and finding the threads of wisdom hidden within.

Wrapping It Up: Chasing Clarity in the Chaos

Throughout this journey, we've peeled back the layers of complexity and unmasked the hidden blind spots within the 3PL landscape. As we wrap up, it's crucial to emphasize the significance of chasing clarity in this chaotic realm. When operating within the intricate web of logistics, it's easy to become entangled in a maze of obscured details and fragmented communications. But amidst this whirlwind, clarity stands as the beacon guiding us through the storm. Let's delve into the essential steps for chasing this elusive clarity. First and foremost, embrace transparency. Shattering the barriers of secrecy and ambiguity will pave the way for clarity to emerge. Open lines of communication, honest discussions, and clear expectations are the pillars upon which transparency is built. Moreover, don't shy away from asking the tough questions. Scrutinize every nook and cranny of your 3PL operations, seeking answers that illuminate the shadows cast by blind spots. Next, cultivate a culture of collaboration. In this interconnected world of logistics, collaborative efforts can unravel complexities and bring forth clarity. Embrace input and perspectives from all stakeholders involved, recognizing that diverse viewpoints often cast light on hidden facets of the operational landscape. Simultaneously, leverage technology to streamline processes and uncover obscured data points. By harnessing the power of advanced tools and systems, you can extract actionable insights while navigating through the chaos. Additionally, be proactive in addressing potential blind spots. Anticipate the twists and turns that may lead to obscurity, and develop contingency plans to address them head-on. Recognize that the pursuit of clarity is not a one-time endeavor but an ongoing commitment. Lastly, empower your team to champion a culture of clarity. Equip them with the knowledge and resources necessary to identify and mitigate blind spots, fostering an environment where clarity is valued and pursued collectively. As we reach the culmination of our exploration, remember that clarity is not merely a destination but an ongoing expedition. The journey of chasing clarity in the chaos requires diligence, adaptability, and a steadfast commitment to unraveling the veils of obscurity within the realm of 3PL. With each step taken towards clarity, the once daunting maze of blind spots begins to unravel, unveiling a landscape ripe with strategic insights and newfound opportunities.

Logistics In The Blind Spot: Finding The Costs You Don't See

The People Problem

Hey, Who's In Charge Here?

In any organization, it's crucial to have a clear understanding of who is responsible for what. When leadership roles are ambiguous or undefined, chaos can ensue. Imagine a ship sailing without a captain at the helm – everyone might be working hard, but if there's no one steering the ship, disaster is inevitable. The same goes for any business or team. Without clear leadership and defined roles, uncertainty reigns, and productivity suffers. It's like trying to play a game with constantly changing rules; no one knows what they're supposed to be doing. This leads to frustration, conflict, and wasted effort. All too often, employees find themselves asking, 'Who's in charge here?' It's not a sign of insubordination, but rather a cry for guidance and direction. Clear leadership roles must be established to provide a framework for decision-making, problem-solving, and accountability. When everyone knows who's responsible for what, trust and efficiency increase, and goals become achievable. In an environment where leadership roles are crystal clear, individuals know where to turn for support and direction. They understand their own responsibilities and how their work fits into the bigger picture. This clarity fosters a sense of ownership and empowerment, as each person can take pride in their contribution and see how it impacts the overall success of the team or organization. Without this clarity, employees may feel adrift, unsure of their purpose and place within the company. This lack of direction can lead to disengagement, dissatisfaction, and ultimately, turnover. Effective leadership is not just about making decisions and giving orders; it's about providing a vision, setting expectations, and creating a supportive structure that enables everyone to thrive. When roles are clearly defined, employees can focus on their tasks with confidence, knowing that their leaders are there to provide guidance and support. This, in turn, paves the way for innovation, collaboration, and a positive work culture. The next time someone asks, 'Who's in charge here?' the answer should be resoundingly clear, ensuring a smooth and efficient operation.

When Roles Are as Clear as Mud

Ever found yourself in a situation where everyone seems to think someone else is responsible for a task, and no one ends up taking charge? That's what happens in organizations where roles are ambiguous or overlapping. When there's no clear definition of who does what, it's like navigating through murky waters with no map or compass. Chaos can reign, finger-pointing becomes the norm, and productivity takes a nosedive. Picture this: you're in a meeting discussing an important project, and when it comes time to assign tasks, everyone looks at each other with confusion. "I thought you were handling that," one person says. "Well, I assumed it was your responsibility," another chimes in. This lack of clarity creates frustration, tension, and ultimately, a lack of progress. Without well-defined roles, teams can end up duplicating efforts, stepping on each other's toes, or worse, neglecting essential tasks altogether. It's not just about assigning titles; it's about ensuring that each member knows exactly what they are responsible for and how their role contributes to the overall success of the organization. Clarity in roles cultivates accountability, fosters teamwork, and empowers individuals to take ownership of their contributions. Clear delineation of responsibilities also streamlines decision-making processes, as everyone knows who should be involved and when. Organizations must actively work towards defining, communicating, and constantly refining roles to ensure alignment and efficiency. Through effective job descriptions, orientation programs, and ongoing communication, employees can gain a clear understanding of their roles, expectations, and the bigger picture, preventing them from feeling lost in the shuffle. One way to tackle this is by conducting regular check-ins to clarify any uncertainties and address evolving needs. By providing consistent feedback and support, leaders can pave the way for a culture where everyone is crystal clear on their part in steering the ship toward success.

Communication: The Game of Telephone

Effective communication is the lifeblood of any successful organization. It's like playing the childhood game of telephone, where one person whispers a message to another and it gets passed along a line of people. But in the business world, it's not just about making sure the message doesn't get lost or distorted along the way; it's also about ensuring that everyone is on the same page, working towards the same goals, and understanding their roles and responsibilities. When communication breaks down, problems arise. It's not just the big, obvious breakdowns that cause trouble; sometimes even the little hiccups can lead to major headaches. Ever sent an email that was misinterpreted, or had a conversation that left both parties confused? That's the game of telephone at play in the business world. The problem is compounded in the context of third-party logistics (3PL), where different teams, departments, and even partner organizations may be involved. Clear and effective communication becomes even more critical. Miscommunication leads to errors, delays, and frustration. It can impact the entire supply chain, from procurement to delivery. But it's not just about the spoken or written word; non-verbal communication also plays a huge role. From body language to the tone of an email, everything sends a message, intentional or not. So, how do we combat this game of telephone? Firstly, it requires setting clear expectations and ensuring that all parties involved understand their roles and responsibilities. Regular check-ins, feedback loops, and open channels of communication are essential. Training in effective communication skills is crucial, helping employees understand how to transmit, receive, and interpret messages accurately. Establishing a culture of transparency and accountability can help minimize misunderstandings. Instituting standard processes for communication, whether it's through formal documentation or digital platforms, provides a structured framework for information flow. Above all, communication needs to be a priority at every level of the organization. Leaders need to model effective communication, and encourage dialogue throughout the company. By addressing the challenges of the game of telephone head-on, we can transform it into a symphony of clear, cohesive communication that drives success and collaboration.

Training? What's That Again?

Many companies overlook the importance of training when it comes to their 3PL operations. "Training? What's That Again?" may sound like a flippant question, but it highlights a critical issue that plagues many logistics operations. Without proper training, your team may be left adrift in a sea of complex processes, struggling to navigate without a compass. Training provides your staff with the knowledge and skills they need to excel in their roles. It empowers them to understand the intricacies of the supply chain, familiarize themselves with the latest technologies, and adapt to ever-changing industry standards. Effective training also fosters confidence, instilling a sense of ownership and purpose in your workforce. When employees feel capable and valued, they are more likely to go above and beyond to deliver outstanding results. Moreover, investing in training demonstrates a commitment to employee development, which can enhance staff retention and loyalty. By neglecting training, you risk creating a workforce that lacks direction, comprehension, and motivation, ultimately hindering your 3PL success. Embracing a culture of continuous learning and improvement is essential for staying ahead in the competitive logistics landscape. Organizations that prioritize training cultivate a knowledgeable, adaptable, and cohesive workforce, capable of overcoming challenges and seizing opportunities. In the next chapter, we'll delve into the often overlooked 'Ghost Shift: Staffing Issues' and explore how to effectively navigate this common obstacle in 3PL operations.

The Ghost Shift: Staffing Issues

Ever heard of the ghost shift? It's not some spooky tale from a horror movie, but rather a real and tangible issue within many organizations. In the world of logistics and 3PL operations, the ghost shift refers to those times when there's a glaring absence of staff where they're sorely needed. Picture this: it's like a scene from a Western movie, with a tumbleweed blowing through an abandoned ghost town. But instead of a deserted saloon, it's your distribution center that's eerily quiet. This staffing shortfall can wreak havoc on your operations, causing delays, errors, and customer dissatisfaction. So, what causes these ghost shifts? There are several factors at play. Sometimes it's poor forecasting or scheduling that leaves critical areas understaffed. Other times, it's high turnover rates that constantly leave you short-handed. Then there are the dreaded unplanned absences due to illness, family emergencies, or other unforeseen circumstances. All these culminate in a perfect storm, leading to operational inefficiencies and potentially costly mistakes. And let's not forget the impact on the staff who do show up for work. They're often left picking up the slack, leading to burnout and decreased morale. But fear not, dear reader, for there are strategies to exorcise these spectral staffing issues. It starts with proactive workforce planning and forecasting to ensure you have the right people, in the right place, at the right time. Implementing cross-training programs can also help in mitigating the effects of unexpected staff shortages. Additionally, fostering an inclusive and supportive work culture can reduce turnover and absenteeism, creating a more reliable and engaged team. Moreover, leveraging technology to streamline processes and automate routine tasks can alleviate the burden on your workforce. By addressing these ghost shifts head-on, you'll banish the specter of understaffing and create a more robust and resilient operation. So, no need to call the ghostbusters – just implement these strategies and watch those ghost shifts fade into the realm of urban legend.

Culture Clash: When Teams Don't Gel

Teams are like ecosystems, and when different individuals with unique backgrounds, work styles, and personalities come together, it can either create a harmonious symphony or a chaotic cacophony. Culture clash within teams can be attributed to a variety of factors, ranging from differences in communication preferences and decision-making approaches to conflicting values and beliefs. In some cases, the clash may stem from varied expectations regarding work ethic, collaboration, and accountability.

One of the most common manifestations of culture clash is the breakdown of effective communication. This breakdown can occur when team members speak different communication languages—metaphorically speaking. While one person might prefer direct, straightforward communication, another might value diplomacy and subtlety. This difference in communication styles can lead to misunderstandings, hurt feelings, and ultimately, a strained working environment.

Moreover, clashes in work styles and problem-solving approaches can impede team effectiveness. Some team members may be more inclined towards risk-taking and quick decision-making, whereas others might lean toward caution and methodical analysis before reaching a consensus. These opposing styles can result in friction and stalled progress. As a result, the team's productivity and overall performance may suffer.

Another key element contributing to culture clash is the diversity of values and beliefs among team members. Individuals from disparate cultural backgrounds, representing different age groups, or hailing from distinct geographical regions may hold differing views on work, ethics, and priorities. These differences can create tension if not addressed constructively and respectfully.

An essential step toward resolving culture clashes within teams involves fostering an open and inclusive environment where diverse perspectives are embraced and celebrated. Providing platforms for team members to share their experiences, understanding, and expectations can aid in bridging the gaps and building mutual respect. Encouraging empathy and active listening can also facilitate better understanding among team members and mitigate potential conflicts.

Additionally, creating structured opportunities for team bonding and collaborative problem-solving initiatives can help break down barriers and foster a more cohesive working dynamic. By engaging in activities that promote teamwork and enhance interpersonal relationships, teams can surpass culture clashes and leverage their diverse skills and insights to drive innovation and shared success.

Motivation Meltdown

Have you ever experienced a time when the team's motivation seemed to hit rock bottom? You know, when everyone seems to be just going through the motions, lacking enthusiasm or passion for their work? This is what we call a 'motivation meltdown.' It's like a dark cloud that hangs over the entire team, casting a shadow on productivity and morale. But why does this happen? There are several factors that can contribute to a motivation meltdown. It could be due to unclear expectations or lack of recognition for a job well done. Sometimes, it's a result of poor leadership or a toxic work environment. When individuals don't feel valued or appreciated, their motivation suffers. Additionally, personal issues or external stressors can seep into the workplace, affecting everyone's drive and focus. So, how do we address a motivation meltdown? First and foremost, communication is key. Leaders need to openly discuss challenges and actively listen to their team members' concerns. Providing regular feedback and acknowledging accomplishments goes a long way in boosting motivation. Creating a positive work culture where every voice is heard and respected can also help prevent motivation meltdowns. On an individual level, finding intrinsic motivation, setting personal goals, and seeking support from colleagues can reignite that spark. Ultimately, overcoming a motivation meltdown requires a collective effort. It's about recognizing the problem, empathizing with each other, and working together to rebuild a sense of purpose and drive. By addressing underlying issues and fostering a supportive, inclusive environment, we can lift the team out of the shadows and into a brighter, more motivated future.

Feedback or the Lack Thereof

Picture this: You're at work, doing your best to get through the day, but you have no idea if what you're doing is meeting expectations. Sound familiar? Feedback, or the lack thereof, can be a major source of frustration for employees. It's like walking in the dark without a flashlight – you stumble around, hoping you're going in the right direction, but never really sure. When feedback is scarce or nonexistent, it leaves employees feeling disconnected and undervalued. This lack of communication can lead to disengagement, decreased morale, and even attrition. Without timely and constructive feedback, how can employees ever know how to improve or where they stand? It's as if they're left stranded on an island with no map or compass. And let's not forget about the impact on performance. When employees are left in the dark about their progress, it's like driving a car with no dashboard – they can't gauge how fast they're going or if they're heading in the right direction. All too often, the absence of feedback leads to missed opportunities for growth and development. But hey, it's not just employees who suffer – the whole organization takes a hit. Without feedback, how can teams collaborate effectively? How can leaders make informed decisions about resource allocation and strategy? The truth is, without feedback, it's difficult to foster a culture of continuous improvement and innovation. But fear not, there is light at the end of the tunnel. Organizations that recognize the value of timely and meaningful feedback cultivate an environment where employees feel heard, valued, and empowered. Constructive feedback provides clarity, promotes accountability, and fuels personal and professional growth. It bridges the gap between where employees are and where they need to be. When feedback becomes a two-way street, communication flourishes, trust strengthens, and individuals thrive. Embracing constructive feedback fosters a culture of transparency and open dialogue. It empowers employees to take ownership of their development and performance, creating a win-win situation for both the individual and the organization. So, the next time you think about holding back on feedback, remember that it's not just a comment – it's a catalyst for growth and success.

Learning to Play Nice

In any organization, fostering an environment where everyone can work together harmoniously is crucial. Learning to play nice isn't just about avoiding conflicts; it's about building a culture of collaboration and respect. This means acknowledging and embracing differences while working towards common goals. To achieve this, leaders must set the tone by demonstrating inclusive behavior and encouraging open communication. Emphasizing the value of diverse perspectives helps create an atmosphere where individuals feel heard and understood. Additionally, providing opportunities for team members to engage in team-building activities and share their personal experiences can foster mutual understanding and empathy. Through active listening and empathy, individuals can learn to appreciate each other's strengths and challenges. Furthermore, cultivating a supportive environment that celebrates achievements and encourages risk-taking fosters a sense of psychological safety. Recognizing and rewarding cooperation and teamwork further reinforces the importance of playing nice. Moreover, instituting clear protocols for conflict resolution and establishing mechanisms for feedback and discussions can mitigate potential sources of discord. Promoting a culture of continuous improvement allows employees to voice their concerns and suggestions, facilitating a sense of ownership and investment in the organization's success. By prioritizing teamwork, organizations can harness the power of collective intelligence and drive innovation. Learning to play nice isn't just a nicety—it's a strategic imperative that empowers individuals and strengthens the fabric of the organization.

Turning People Problems into People Power

In a perfect world, workplace dynamics would always be harmonious. But the reality is that conflicts can arise, personalities clash, and miscommunications happen. Now, instead of viewing these challenges as insurmountable hurdles, it's time to reframe them as opportunities for growth and transformation. Turning people problems into people power involves taking a proactive approach to understanding and addressing the root causes of these issues.

One fundamental step is to foster an environment of open communication. Encourage team members to express their thoughts and concerns freely and respectfully. Active listening is also key—truly understanding each other's perspectives can defuse tensions and build empathy. Establishing transparent and inclusive channels for feedback and dialogue not only resolves immediate conflicts but also strengthens the overall team dynamic.

Moreover, investing in professional development and training can be a game-changer. When individuals are equipped with the necessary skills and knowledge to excel in their roles, they feel empowered and valued. By recognizing and harnessing the unique strengths of each team member, leaders can transform any existing friction into a powerful force for collaboration and innovation.

Building a positive company culture should be a non-negotiable priority. Lead by example, and cultivate an atmosphere of respect, trust, and support among colleagues. Recognize and celebrate achievements, fostering a sense of belonging and pride. A strong sense of unity not only minimizes conflicts but also emboldens individuals to confront and resolve any issues that do arise.

To truly turn people problems into people power, create opportunities for team members to engage in meaningful projects, collaborative problem-solving, and decision-making processes. Empower them to take ownership and responsibility, instilling a sense of investment in the collective success of the organization.

Lastly, remember that fostering people power requires ongoing effort. Periodically evaluate the team dynamics, address any emerging issues promptly, and continue to refine the strategies for enhancing collaboration and harmony. By nurturing a culture that transforms adversities into strengths, organizations can unlock the immense potential within their human capital, propelling towards collective excellence.

Logistics In The Blind Spot: Finding The Costs You Don't See

Process Inefficiencies

Understanding the Ground Zero of Bottlenecks

Let's dive into common reasons bottlenecks occur and how they can be spotted before they halt progress. In the world of logistics and supply chain management, bottlenecks are often cited as one of the biggest obstacles to smooth operations. These slowdowns can occur at various points in the process, leading to delays, increased costs, and frustrated customers. Identifying the ground zero of bottlenecks is crucial for streamlining operations and maximizing efficiency. Bottlenecks can stem from a variety of sources, such as limited resources, outdated technology, or inefficient processes. By gaining a deep understanding of these root causes, businesses can proactively address potential bottlenecks before they escalate into critical issues. One common cause of bottlenecks is inadequate resource allocation. This could include insufficient staffing, equipment, or space to handle the volume of goods passing through a particular point in the supply chain. Identifying these resource constraints early on allows organizations to make the necessary adjustments to prevent bottlenecks from occurring. Additionally, outdated technology and systems can create bottlenecks by slowing down processes, causing errors, and increasing lead times. It's essential to evaluate the technology infrastructure regularly and invest in upgrades where needed to ensure smooth operations. Inefficient processes can also serve as breeding grounds for bottlenecks. When certain steps in the supply chain are prone to delays, errors, or redundancies, they can create chokepoints that impede the flow of goods. By analyzing the workflow and eliminating inefficiencies, organizations can preemptively address potential bottlenecks. Recognizing the warning signs of impending bottlenecks is equally important. Key indicators may include increased wait times, backlogs in production, or rising error rates. Monitoring these metrics and being vigilant about potential bottlenecks can enable proactive problem-solving and prevent disruptions in the supply chain. Ultimately, understanding the ground zero of bottlenecks involves a comprehensive evaluation of resources, technology, and processes. By taking a proactive approach to identifying and addressing potential bottlenecks, businesses can optimize their operations, enhance customer satisfaction, and maintain a competitive edge in the market.

Identifying Where Time Slips Away

In the world of logistics, time is money. But all too often, time slips away unnoticed, eroding efficiency and sapping profitability. In this section, we delve into the hidden crevices where precious minutes evaporate, leaving businesses grappling with lost opportunities and mounting costs. From the moment a shipment enters the system to its final delivery, every step along the way harbors potential time drains. Perhaps it's a delay in documentation processing at the receiving dock, or an avoidable hold-up during order picking due to poor inventory organization. These seemingly minor inefficiencies can snowball into significant time losses that impact overall operations. What's crucial is not just identifying these instances but understanding their root causes. It could be a lack of standardized processes leading to inconsistent handling across different locations, or inadequate training resulting in workforce inefficiency. Sometimes, external factors such as unreliable transportation providers or unexpected customs delays further compound the issue. Through real-world examples and detailed analysis, we'll uncover the telltale signs of time slipping through the cracks, shedding light on why these occurrences occur and how they can be rectified. By focusing on where time escapes us, businesses can regain control over their operations, ensuring that every minute is utilized to its fullest potential. Be it through process reengineering, technological interventions, or a shift in operational paradigms, the pursuit of efficiency begins with pinpointing where time is lost and resolving to make every second count.

Case Studies: Lessons from Unruly Processes

In the world of logistics, there are countless examples of unruly processes wreaking havoc on a company's efficiency and bottom line. These case studies serve as invaluable lessons that shed light on the dire consequences of unchecked inefficiencies.

Take the case of a mid-sized distribution company that grappled with a labyrinthine order fulfillment process. What started as a minor bottleneck at the receiving dock cascaded into major delays throughout the entire warehouse. This resulted in a domino effect of missed delivery deadlines, dissatisfied customers, and ultimately, financial losses. By dissecting this scenario, we can discern how small inefficiencies can snowball into operational nightmares.

Furthermore, let's delve into the account of a global manufacturer whose inventory management system failed to keep pace with their rapid expansion. The ensuing confusion and errors led to overstocking of slow-moving items while creating shortages of critical products. The repercussions were felt across their supply chain and beyond, leading to strained relationships with key partners and severe reputational damage. These case studies emphasize the paramount importance of streamlined processes in maintaining a competitive edge.

Another compelling example arises from a transportation company that struggled with disorganized communication channels. This resulted in missed pickups, misrouted shipments, and an inundation of customer complaints. The fallout included increased operating costs, decreased customer satisfaction, and a tarnished brand image. These real-world instances underscore the pivotal role of efficient communication in the seamless functioning of logistics operations.

Each of these case studies offers a wealth of insights into the complexities of modern supply chain management, highlighting the tangible impacts of process inefficiencies. By understanding the root causes and multifaceted effects of these issues, organizations can proactively implement measures to preempt similar challenges. These stories prompt us to reevaluate our own operational frameworks, urging us to strive for precision and coherence in our processes to avoid falling victim to the same pitfalls.

Communication Breakdowns: The Silent Productivity Killers

Effective communication is the lifeblood of any well-oiled logistics operation. But in the complex web of supply chain management, breakdowns in communication can be the silent productivity killers that wreak havoc on efficiency and customer satisfaction. Whether it's a missed email, a misunderstood instruction, or a lack of clarity in reporting, communication breakdowns can lead to delays, errors, and frustration throughout the entire process. These issues often go unnoticed until they snowball into major problems, causing costly disruptions and tarnishing the reputation of your logistics operation. The root causes of communication breakdowns can stem from various sources, including ambiguous instructions, lack of accountability, or simply not listening attentively. One common issue is assuming that messages have been received and understood without confirming it, leading to misunderstandings and mistakes. Additionally, the use of outdated or convoluted communication channels can hinder the flow of crucial information, slowing down operations and creating unnecessary bottlenecks. Furthermore, poor communication can also strain relationships with partners and customers, as misunderstandings and discrepancies erode trust and create dissatisfaction. To combat these silent productivity killers, it's crucial to implement clear communication protocols and foster a culture of open dialogue within your logistics team. This may involve setting up regular check-ins, using standardized templates for documentation, and providing comprehensive training on effective communication practices. Additionally, leveraging digital tools and platforms for real-time collaboration and information sharing can streamline communication and reduce the likelihood of misunderstandings. It's also essential to establish clear lines of accountability and ensure that all team members understand their roles and responsibilities in the communication process. By addressing communication breakdowns head-on, you can mitigate the risks they pose to your logistics operations and pave the way for smoother, more efficient processes. Recognizing the impact of silent productivity killers like communication breakdowns is the first step toward building a resilient and high-performing logistics operation.

Why Haste Makes Waste in Logistics

In the fast-paced world of logistics, it's easy to get caught up in the hustle and bustle of meeting tight deadlines and ensuring that everything is moving smoothly. However, what often gets overlooked in this frenzy is the detrimental impact of haste on overall efficiency and long-term success. When the pressure to meet unrealistic timeframes becomes the priority, errors are more likely to occur. Whether it's inaccurate data entry, rushed quality checks, or hasty decision-making, each instance has the potential to create a domino effect of setbacks throughout the supply chain. These small errors may seem insignificant in the moment, but they can lead to significant delays, increased costs, and ultimately dissatisfied customers. Moreover, the rush to complete tasks can result in overlooked opportunities for process optimization and improvement. Instead of taking the time to identify where bottlenecks exist and developing sustainable solutions, hasty actions perpetuate a cycle of inefficiency. Furthermore, the toll of haste extends beyond operational missteps; it also impacts the well-being of employees. Constant pressure to expedite processes can lead to burnout, decreased morale, and even higher turnover rates, ultimately hindering the organization's ability to retain skilled talent. As such, it's crucial for logistics professionals to recognize that haste not only leads to waste in terms of resources and time but also jeopardizes the overall health of the business. Embracing a mindset that prioritizes thoroughness over speed offers the opportunity to uncover hidden efficiencies, enhance accuracy, and cultivate a work environment that supports sustainable success. By acknowledging the pitfalls of haste, businesses can proactively implement strategies to mitigate these risks and lay the foundation for long-term prosperity.

The Ripple Effect of Small Errors

In the intricate dance of logistics, small errors can have significant consequences. Picture this: a mislabeled package sitting innocently on a shelf, waiting to be shipped out. The address is slightly off, the barcode ambiguous. This seemingly benign mistake sets off a chain reaction of inefficiency. A picker pulls the wrong item, causing confusion in the warehouse. As a result, an incorrect order ships out, prompting customer dissatisfaction and costly returns. And there it is—the ripple effect.

It's not just physical errors that propagate through the system; misinformation and miscommunication are equally culpable. A vague instruction from a supervisor can lead to misunderstood directives, creating chaos downstream. Perhaps a slight misinterpretation of a process guideline causes undue delay or suboptimal performance. These tiny discrepancies may seem insignificant at first, but their cumulative impact can be staggering.

Consider the domino effect of delayed shipments. Simple inattention at one stage ripples through the supply chain, affecting inventory levels, production schedules, and ultimately, customer satisfaction. One snag in a fulfillment center can reverberate across the entire network, disrupting the delicate balance of operations and eroding trust with clients. Even minor slips in accuracy can snowball into major setbacks for your business.

This ripple effect highlights the interconnected nature of logistics—every action or oversight has repercussions. However, rather than succumb to despair, take heart in the realization that the converse is also true. Addressing small errors can yield disproportionately large improvements. By paying attention to detail, tightening processes, and refining communication, you can carve out substantial gains. Keep in mind that even the tiniest pebble thrown into a pond creates ripples. Likewise, rectifying small errors can send positive reverberations throughout your entire logistical framework, enhancing efficiency and fortifying customer relationships.

Simple Fixes with Big Impacts

In the world of logistics and supply chain management, it's often the seemingly inconsequential details that can make or break operations. The good news is that these small errors are also where simple fixes can yield significant improvements. Let's delve into some examples of these impactful adjustments that have the potential to revolutionize your processes without requiring a complete overhaul. One common area for improvement is in inventory management. When items are inaccurately labeled, misplaced, or poorly categorized, it can lead to a cascade of issues downstream. Implementing a more precise labeling system and organized storage layout can result in reduced picking errors and faster fulfillment times. Another remarkably effective yet often overlooked fix is streamlining communication channels. Miscommunication or lack of clarity between team members and departments can create bottlenecks that impede smooth operations. By introducing clearer protocols and fostering a culture of open dialogue, you can sidestep a host of unnecessary delays and errors. Furthermore, embracing automation and technology can significantly streamline various processes. Whether it's automating routine data entry tasks, or implementing a robust warehouse management system, investing in technology can lead to a drastic reduction in manual errors and an increase in overall efficiency. Another area ripe for impactful change is in the realm of supplier relationships. Establishing transparent and collaborative partnerships with suppliers can minimize delays and discrepancies, ultimately leading to smoother operations. Moreover, by conducting regular reviews and audits of vendor performance, you can identify areas for improvement and negotiate better terms. Finally, a critical but often undervalued fix is employee training and empowerment. Providing comprehensive training programs and giving employees the autonomy to make decisions within set parameters can result in improved morale, reduced errors, and amplified productivity. These simple fixes, when applied strategically, can produce far-reaching impacts on your logistical and operational capabilities, helping you to achieve greater efficiencies and ultimately improving your bottom line.

The Role of Transparency in Smoothing Operations

Transparency within the logistics industry is akin to a beacon guiding a vessel safely through rough waters. It not only fosters trust between partners but also plays a pivotal role in streamlining operations. When all parties involved have a clear view of the entire supply chain process, it becomes easier to pinpoint inefficiencies and alleviate bottlenecks. Moreover, transparency helps to minimize misunderstandings, allowing for proactive solutions to be implemented.

At its core, transparency serves as the foundation for collaboration and problem-solving. By openly sharing information and data, businesses can identify areas where improvements are needed and swiftly address them. This mindset shift from secrecy to openness propels the logistics industry toward greater efficiency and agility. Teams become empowered to make informed decisions, leading to smoother operations and improved overall performance.

From a customer perspective, transparency breeds confidence. When clients are kept apprised of every stage of the logistics process, they feel reassured and valued. Whether it's tracking the movement of their goods or understanding potential delays, customers appreciate being in the loop. Consequently, transparent practices enhance customer satisfaction and loyalty, ultimately benefiting the bottom line.

It's important to note that achieving transparency isn't solely about technology and data sharing. While advanced tracking systems and real-time reporting are invaluable, fostering a culture of transparency requires open communication and a commitment to honesty. This cultural shift toward transparency should permeate the entire organization, from leadership down to frontline workers. Only then can the true benefits of transparency be realized.

In essence, the role of transparency in smoothing operations cannot be overstated. It acts as the adhesive that binds all facets of the supply chain together, ensuring that each component operates harmoniously. By embracing transparency, businesses unlock the potential for continuous improvement, enhanced relationships, and sustainable growth.

Aligning Processes with Business Goals

In the fast-paced world of logistics, aligning processes with business goals is essential for sustainable growth and competitive advantage. It's not just about moving goods from point A to point B; it's about doing so in a way that supports the overarching strategic vision of the organization. To achieve this alignment, it's crucial to start by gaining a deep understanding of the core objectives and priorities of the business. What are the key performance indicators (KPIs) that drive decision-making? How does the company define success, and what metrics are used to measure progress? Once these questions are answered, it becomes possible to map out the specific processes and workflows that directly impact these goals. This involves a comprehensive review of current practices and an honest assessment of their effectiveness. Are there any bottlenecks or inefficiencies that hinder the achievement of strategic objectives? Are there redundant steps that can be eliminated to streamline operations? Armed with this insight, the next step is to realign processes to better serve the bigger picture. This may involve redefining standard operating procedures, implementing new technologies, or even restructuring teams to optimize efficiency. Moreover, an emphasis on continuous improvement becomes paramount. Processes cannot be static; they must evolve in tandem with the evolving needs of the business. Alignment with business goals also demands a cultural shift within the organization. It requires all stakeholders to understand how their daily activities contribute to the larger mission and to take ownership of driving progress toward overarching targets. This may necessitate training and education initiatives to ensure everyone is equipped with the knowledge and skills needed to execute their roles with a strategic mindset. Ultimately, achieving synchronization between operational processes and business objectives is a journey, not a destination. It requires ongoing vigilance, adaptability, and a commitment to staying attuned to the ever-changing landscape of the industry. When done effectively, the payoff is significant – enhanced agility, improved customer satisfaction, and a stronger position in the market. By aligning processes with business goals, companies can transform their logistics operations from mere support functions to strategic differentiators that propel them toward sustained success.

Setting the Stage for Seamless Tech Integration

When it comes to the intersection of technology and logistics, seamless integration is the key to unlocking a world of efficiency. This section explores the crucial steps in preparing your business for a smooth technological integration that harmonizes with your operational ecosystem. The first step in setting the stage for seamless tech integration is to conduct a comprehensive analysis of your current technology landscape and how it aligns with your overall business objectives. This involves assessing your existing systems, identifying any potential gaps or redundancies, and evaluating their capabilities to support the future growth and scalability of your operations. By gaining a clear understanding of your technology infrastructure, you can pinpoint areas that require enhancement or consolidation to pave the way for a cohesive integration. Next, it's essential to define your integration goals and priorities. Understand the specific pain points and inefficiencies that you aim to address through tech integration, whether it's streamlining order processing, optimizing inventory management, or improving real-time visibility across the supply chain. Prioritizing these goals will guide the selection of technologies and solutions that best align with your strategic objectives. With a solid grasp of your existing technology landscape and defined integration goals, the next step involves careful consideration of the available tech solutions. This entails researching and evaluating potential platforms, software, and tools that offer the functionality and compatibility required to seamlessly integrate with your current systems. It's critical to seek solutions that not only meet your immediate needs but also have the flexibility to evolve alongside your business as it grows and evolves. Additionally, engaging with technology providers and industry experts can provide valuable insights into the latest innovations and best practices for successful integration. Once the right tech solutions have been identified, the focus shifts to establishing a robust framework for integration. This involves developing a detailed implementation plan that outlines the sequence of integration activities, allocation of resources, and timelines for deployment. Collaboration between internal stakeholders, IT teams, and external technology partners is pivotal to ensure a coordinated approach that minimizes disruptions to ongoing operations. Moreover, testing and validation procedures should be diligently mapped out to validate the seamless interoperability of newly integrated systems and mitigate any potential risks before full-scale deployment. Finally, the journey towards seamless tech integration culminates in fostering a culture of adaptability and continuous improvement within your organization. Encourage open communication and knowledge-sharing among teams to facilitate a smooth transition and drive user adoption of new technologies. Providing comprehensive training and support resources will empower employees to embrace and leverage the benefits of integrated systems effectively. As advancements in technology continue to shape the logistics landscape, setting the stage for seamless integration becomes an integral part of staying ahead in a competitive market. By embarking on this proactive journey, businesses can position themselves to harness the full potential of technology, elevate operational efficiencies, and ultimately deliver enhanced value to customers.

Logistics In The Blind Spot: Finding The Costs You Don't See

Technology & Integration Gaps

Peeking Behind the Digital Curtain

Digital systems have become an integral part of modern business operations, streamlining processes and connecting various components of the supply chain. However, within these seemingly seamless operations lie hidden complexities that often go unnoticed. The tech talk surrounding digital systems is rife with jargon and lingo that can be daunting for those not intimately familiar with the technological landscape. It's not just about the hardware and software; it's about understanding how these elements interact and impact the overall logistics and fulfillment processes. Peeking behind the digital curtain reveals a web of interconnected systems, each with its own set of intricacies and dependencies. From APIs to cloud-based solutions, the jargon surrounding technology can confound even the most seasoned logistics professionals. Yet, gaining a deeper understanding of this tech talk is crucial for uncovering inefficiencies and unlocking opportunities for improvement. By demystifying the complex terminology, we can begin to bridge the gap between end users and the IT teams responsible for maintaining these digital infrastructures. Exploring the nuances of digital systems also sheds light on the potential points of failure and bottlenecks that may hinder operational efficiency. Moreover, delving into the digital realm allows us to grasp the implications of outdated technologies and the pressing need for integration with modern solutions. As we venture further into this digital domain, we'll navigate through the labyrinth of acronyms, protocols, and interfaces, equipping ourselves with the knowledge needed to make informed decisions regarding technology investments and optimizations. Ultimately, by peeking behind the digital curtain, we stand poised to harness the transformative power of technology while understanding and mitigating its inherent complexities.

The Tech Talk: Jargon and Lingo

In the world of logistics technology, there's a whole new language to learn. It can feel like you need a glossary just to keep up with the acronyms and tech jargon thrown around in conversations. From WMS (Warehouse Management System) to TMS (Transportation Management System), and from EDI (Electronic Data Interchange) to API (Application Programming Interface), it's like the alphabet soup of the digital world. But understanding this tech talk is crucial for navigating the landscape of logistics technology. Once you start speaking the language, you'll find that communication with tech providers becomes clearer, enabling you to make more informed decisions. Learning about these terms and concepts doesn't have to be overwhelming - we'll break down the key terminology and explain what it means for your business. Moreover, we'll explore real-world examples to put the jargon into context, making it easier for you to see how these technologies impact day-to-day operations. By demystifying the tech talk and shedding light on the lingo, you'll gain the confidence to engage in meaningful discussions about the technology that powers your logistics operations. Ultimately, our goal is to empower you with the knowledge to evaluate, implement, and leverage technology effectively, ensuring that you stay ahead of the curve in an ever-evolving digital world.

Integrations: The Missing Puzzle Piece

In the world of logistics, the success of any operation hinges on seamless integrations. Think of it like assembling a complex jigsaw puzzle—each piece needs to fit perfectly to reveal the bigger picture. When we talk about technology & integration gaps, this is where the rubber meets the road. Integrations serve as the vital link between different systems, allowing data to flow smoothly and ensuring that every part of the process works in harmony. But what happens when this crucial puzzle piece goes missing? The consequences can be far-reaching, impacting everything from operational efficiency to customer satisfaction.

One of the primary challenges lies in bridging the gap between legacy systems and modern technological advancements. While older systems might have served their purpose in the past, they can now create roadblocks to achieving streamlined operations. These outdated technologies often lack the capacity to communicate with newer platforms, leaving critical data siloed and processes fragmented. The result? Missed opportunities, increased errors, and bottlenecks that hinder progress.

But integrations are about more than just connecting the dots between software applications. They also play a pivotal role in uniting people, processes, and technology. Picture a scenario where a state-of-the-art warehouse management system doesn't sync with the transportation management platform, leading to inefficiencies in tracking inventory movement and coordinating shipments. It's not just a matter of digitizing processes; it's about creating an interconnected ecosystem where each element supports the other seamlessly.

Realizing the gravity of this issue, the industry is actively seeking solutions to bridge these integration gaps. Whether through standardized APIs, middleware solutions, or custom-built connectors, the aim is to establish interoperability between disparate systems. Yet, the journey towards comprehensive integrations is riddled with real stories and struggles. Many logistics professionals have faced the uphill battle of making dissimilar technologies speak the same language, discovering that even small tweaks can make a world of difference. The key here is recognizing that integrations aren't a one-time fix, but an ongoing commitment to fine-tuning the puzzle until every piece falls into place.

So, as we delve deeper into the intricacies of integrations, let's explore the challenges, triumphs, and strategies behind overcoming technology & integration gaps. Through harnessing the power of seamless connections and nurturing a holistic approach to technology adoption, we pave the way toward operational excellence and unlock the true potential of logistics in the digital era.

Old Systems, New Problems

So, we've talked about integrations being the missing puzzle piece in our 3PL tech setup. But what about the systems that have been running the show for years? Yes, those old faithful systems that have served you well and have become an integral part of your operations. While they may have been your go-to solutions for a long time, they could be causing more problems than you realize. Let's delve into the potential issues that can arise from relying on outdated systems. Firstly, compatibility becomes a concern. Newer technologies and software may not play well with these older systems, leading to integration headaches and potential breakdowns in communication. Security risks also rear their ugly heads when dealing with old systems. These systems might not have the necessary updates and patches to keep them secure from modern cyber threats, leaving your sensitive data vulnerable. Maintenance becomes another headache. When something goes wrong with an old system, finding support and spare parts can be a real challenge. This can lead to prolonged downtime and increased costs. Moreover, the lack of flexibility in adapting to changing business needs is a significant drawback of older systems. As your business evolves, your systems need to keep pace, but old systems may struggle to meet your new requirements. Staff productivity can also take a hit when working with outdated systems. The clunky interfaces and slow performance can frustrate employees, impacting their efficiency. And let's not forget about the missed opportunities for innovation and improvement that come from sticking with the status quo. It's clear that holding on to old systems can create a host of new problems, adding to the existing challenges of navigating 3PL technology and integration gaps. Fortunately, understanding these issues is the first step in addressing them, and in the upcoming section, we'll explore how to bridge the gap between old and new, ensuring that your systems work harmoniously to support your operations.

When Technology Fails the Human Touch

Technology has undoubtedly revolutionized the supply chain industry, streamlining processes, and enhancing efficiency in ways we could have never imagined. However, amidst all the buzz surrounding cutting-edge technologies, it's crucial to remember the indispensable value of the human touch. When technology takes center stage, there's a risk of losing sight of the personal connections and intuitive responses that only humans can provide. We've all experienced those moments when an automated response or a glitch in a system left us feeling frustrated and unheard. Whether it's a missed deadline notification sent by a robot or an impersonal email lacking empathy, there's no denying that technology, despite its many benefits, can sometimes fall short in addressing the nuanced needs of individuals. The real challenge lies in finding the delicate balance between technological advancements and preserving the human touch. It's about recognizing that while technology can optimize processes, it's the human element that breathes life and understanding into every interaction. One cannot replace the other, but rather, they should complement each other harmoniously. More than just a cog in the machine, employees bring unique insights, emotional intelligence, and adaptability that technology simply cannot replicate. Whether it's managing unexpected disruptions or fostering meaningful relationships with clients, the human touch remains an irreplaceable asset. As we navigate this increasingly digital landscape, it becomes imperative to ensure that technology serves to enhance our human capabilities rather than overshadow them. A successful supply chain doesn't solely depend on state-of-the-art systems; it thrives on the collaboration between technology and empowered, empathetic individuals. Moreover, recognizing when technology fails the human touch opens up an opportunity for growth and improvement. By acknowledging these shortcomings, we pave the way for innovative solutions that bridge the gap between automation and personalized service. Ultimately, it's not a question of choosing between technology and the human touch; it's about harnessing the power of both to create a supply chain that is efficient, responsive, and deeply human.

Bridging the Gap: How to Connect It All

When it comes to navigating the intricate landscape of technology and integration within the realm of logistics, there's a critical need for strategies that effectively bridge the gap between systems and processes. In today's fast-paced world, the ability to seamlessly connect different technologies is essential for staying competitive and meeting customer demands. But achieving this cohesion isn't without its hurdles. This section sheds light on practical approaches to overcoming the challenges of integration and building a more harmonious tech ecosystem. We'll explore how to assess current technology gaps and identify areas for improvement, offering real-life examples and success stories from industry leaders who have managed to successfully bridge their own digital divides. Moreover, we will dive into the nuances of integrating legacy systems with modern platforms and the inherent complexities involved. From establishing clear communication channels between disparate technologies to implementing scalable solutions, we'll provide actionable insights and best practices to help readers craft a roadmap towards holistic integration. Along the way, we'll emphasize the importance of fostering an organizational culture that embraces adaptability and innovation, encouraging a mindset that continuously seeks to bridge both technological and operational gaps. By the end of this chapter, readers will not only have gained a deeper understanding of the integration process but will also be equipped with practical tools and knowledge to confidently navigate their own technological landscapes.

Real Stories, Real Struggles with Integration

Real-life accounts of businesses facing integration challenges reveal the often underestimated complexities that pertain to technology and system interoperability within the logistics domain. These narratives paint a vivid picture of the struggles faced by companies striving to enhance collaboration and efficiency while grappling with diverse platforms and data silos. One telling story highlights the profound impact of inadequate integration: a mid-sized e-commerce retailer, in a bid to streamline operations, implemented a cutting-edge inventory management system without seamlessly integrating it with their existing order fulfillment software. Result? A logistical nightmare characterized by inaccurate stock levels, delayed orders, and frustrated customers. Another case underscores the intricacies of API integrations as a small manufacturer finds itself entangled in the quagmire of incompatible systems, leading to costly double data entry and a compromised customer experience. These anecdotes underscore the genuine obstacles encountered when navigating the integration landscape, illuminating the need for meticulous planning and comprehensive alignment of technologies. By presenting these real-world scenarios, we gain valuable insights into the multifaceted nature of integration roadblocks—elevating our understanding beyond theoretical discourse and offering tangible lessons rooted in practical experience.

Little Tweaks, Big Differences

In the intricate world of logistics and supply chain management, small adjustments can often yield significant results. Whether it's streamlining a communication process or fine-tuning an existing technology solution, the compounding impact of these seemingly minor changes can be transformative. This section delves into the concept that little tweaks can lead to big differences in the performance of your 3PL operations. Consider this scenario: An organization implementing a slight modification in their inventory tracking system, resulting in a reduction of errors by 30% and a noticeable boost in operational efficiency. The ripple effect of such tweaks extends beyond the immediate operational improvements; it also affects customer satisfaction, vendor relations, and overall bottom-line performance. Even minor modifications to the workflow, when strategically identified and carefully implemented, can lead to notable enhancements in reliability, accuracy, and speed. We'll explore case studies of companies that recognized the power of little tweaks, and how they achieved substantial gains by focusing on optimizing small details. Moreover, we'll examine the behavioral and cultural aspects of embracing a mindset that values continuous improvement at every level of the organization. As we navigate through this section, keep in mind that even the smallest adjustment, if targeted and executed with precision, has the potential to make a monumental impact on the efficiency and competitiveness of your 3PL operation.

Future-Proofing Your Tech Setup

As the business landscape continues to evolve at an unprecedented pace, the importance of future-proofing your tech setup becomes increasingly evident. Future-proofing is not just about finding the latest and greatest technologies; it's about ensuring that your systems and processes can adapt and scale alongside your business. In this section, we'll explore strategies for future-proofing your tech setup to stay ahead of the curve.

One crucial aspect of future-proofing is staying abreast of emerging technologies. This involves actively monitoring industry trends, attending relevant conferences, and engaging with thought leaders in the field. By keeping a finger on the pulse of technological advancements, you can identify opportunities to integrate new solutions that enhance efficiency and performance.

Embracing flexibility is another key component of future-proofing your tech setup. Your systems should be designed to accommodate changes and upgrades without disrupting core operations. This may involve investing in modular architectures and scalable infrastructure that can easily adapt to evolving business requirements.

Furthermore, it's essential to prioritize interoperability when selecting and implementing technology solutions. Seamless integration between different systems and applications is critical for creating a cohesive and efficient tech environment. By fostering interoperability, you can avoid siloed data and functionality, unlocking the full potential of your tech stack.

The concept of future-proofing extends beyond technology alone; it also encompasses cultivating a culture of innovation and adaptability within your organization. Encouraging cross-functional collaboration and empowering employees to experiment with new tools and approaches can foster a dynamic environment where technology evolves in sync with business needs.

Additionally, cybersecurity readiness is an integral part of future-proofing your tech setup. As digital threats become increasingly sophisticated, organizations must proactively implement robust security measures to safeguard their data and systems. This entails conducting regular vulnerability assessments, staying updated on best practices, and investing in advanced security protocols.

Lastly, future-proofing your tech setup necessitates a forward-thinking approach to investment. It's crucial to allocate resources towards long-term sustainability rather than short-term fixes. By making strategic technology investments with a focus on scalability and longevity, you can position your business to thrive amidst technological advancements and disruptive shifts in the market.

In conclusion, future-proofing your tech setup is an ongoing journey that demands proactive planning, continuous learning, and a mindset rooted in adaptability. By embracing emerging technologies, prioritizing flexibility and interoperability, nurturing a culture of innovation, fortifying cybersecurity measures, and making forward-looking investments, you can equip your business with a robust tech foundation that stands the test of time.

Where We Go from Here

Whether you're just starting off in the world of logistics or you've been immersed in it for years, the path forward can sometimes appear daunting. As we navigate through the intricate web of technology and integration gaps, it's crucial to look ahead. The future of logistics and supply chain management is promising, and by staying proactive and adaptable, you can set yourself up for success.

Embracing a forward-thinking mindset involves acknowledging the rapid pace of technological advancements. Innovation isn't slowing down, and neither should we. By keeping a keen eye on emerging technologies and trends, we can ensure that our tech setup remains relevant and efficient. This demands an open-minded approach to change, a willingness to explore new solutions, and an ongoing commitment to learning and development.

Realistically, the road ahead may be filled with obstacles, but they shouldn't deter us. Instead, they should serve as opportunities for growth and improvement. When faced with challenges, the key lies in leveraging our learnings, sharing experiences, and collaborating with industry peers. Engaging in open dialogues about integration struggles, technology hiccups, and potential solutions fosters a collective environment of support and innovation.

As we chart this course, it's essential to recognize the importance of flexibility. Shying away from rigid structures and embracing adaptability enables us to embrace change more readily and navigate any upcoming shifts in the industry. Flexibility also means being open to recalibrating our approaches, strategies, and even our technology infrastructure when necessary.

Moreover, the journey forward invites us to consider the human aspect within our digital landscapes. While technology is undoubtedly pivotal, it shouldn't overshadow the value of human connections and expertise in the logistics realm. Striking a balance between tech solutions and human touchpoints is essential for sustainable progress. Ensuring that our systems are not only efficient but also user-friendly can significantly impact operational outcomes.

The horizon is brimming with possibilities waiting to be explored. By proactively addressing existing gaps, fostering a culture of continuous improvement, and embracing the ever-evolving technological landscape, we can steer logistics and supply chain management toward a future defined by efficiency, connectivity, and innovation.

Logistics In The Blind Spot: Finding The Costs You Don't See

Pricing Models That Hide More Than They Reveal

Hey, What's the Real Cost Here?

Have you ever felt like you were quoted a price for something, only to be hit with additional fees once the bill arrived? It's frustrating, isn't it? In the world of 3PL, add-on fees can be like hidden landmines waiting to explode your budget. At first glance, a service might seem reasonably priced, but once you start uncovering all the extra charges, the true cost becomes alarming.

Take a moment to consider how these fees impact your overall costs. Sure, the base rate might look attractive, but dive deeper and you'll find a laundry list of potential add-ons – storage fees, fuel surcharges, administrative costs, accessorial fees…the list goes on. It's not just about what you're quoted; it's about what you actually end up paying. And those seemingly small add-ons can quickly snowball into a significant part of your expenses.

Moreover, the opacity surrounding these charges makes budgeting and forecasting a real challenge. How can you accurately plan for expenses when you don't know what surprises might be lurking in the fine print? The lack of transparency in fee structures adds an element of uncertainty that can disrupt your financial projections and erode your bottom line.

When assessing the real cost, it's crucial to ask the right questions and demand clarity around all potential fees. Ensure that your 3PL provider is upfront about their pricing model and can clearly articulate any possible additional charges. Ignoring this critical step could spell financial disaster down the road. Trust me, the devil is in the details, and in the case of 3PL pricing, it's essential to bring those details into the light if you want to avoid costly surprises.

The Sneaky World of Add-On Fees

Ever felt like you were getting a good deal, only to be blindsided by unexpected charges? The world of 3PL add-on fees can feel like navigating a maze in the dark. It's not just about the base rate for services; there's a whole universe of additional costs lurking around every corner. These extras can quickly balloon your expenses and throw your budget into disarray. But fear not – armed with knowledge, you can navigate these treacherous waters and emerge victorious. Let's shine a light on some of the most common sneaky add-on fees that 3PLs may try to slip under the radar.

First up, there's the notorious accessorial charges. These are the sneaky fees tacked on for any extra services beyond the standard pick-up and delivery. Everything from liftgate usage to inside deliveries can come with a hefty price tag attached, catching many unsuspecting businesses off guard. Then there's the storage fees – if your goods spend a little too long in the warehouse, get ready to fork out even more money. And don't forget about those reclassification charges; one small mistake in categorizing your freight, and suddenly you're facing a whole new set of fees. Oh, and let's not overlook fuel surcharges – because why should the fluctuating cost of diesel fall solely on the shoulders of the 3PL?

But 3PLs aren't done yet. You might also encounter detention charges for delays, expedited service fees for when you need something yesterday, and even paperwork processing fees for the pleasure of bureaucracy. It's a minefield out there, and it can have a real impact on your bottom line. All these add-ons can make comparing quotes a nightmare, as you try to decipher which fees are included and which will sneak up on you later. And as much as we'd like to believe in the kindness of our 3PL partners, it's important to remember that these fees often represent a significant source of revenue for them.

Navigating the elusive world of add-on fees involves much more than triple-checking an invoice. It requires a deeper understanding of your specific needs, clear communication with your 3PL provider, and a firm grasp on industry standards. We'll delve into strategies for identifying, negotiating, and managing these fees – ensuring that you remain in control of your logistics costs and avoid falling victim to the shadowy underworld of add-on charges.

Decoding Freight Charges

Freight charges are the backbone of the logistics industry, but decoding them can sometimes feel like unraveling a complex puzzle. When you ship goods, there's more to the cost than just the transportation itself. It involves understanding the various elements that contribute to freight charges, and these can include factors such as fuel surcharges, accessorial fees, and dimensional weight pricing. Fuel surcharges are often applied to offset fluctuations in fuel prices, and they can catch you off guard if you're not aware of how they are calculated or negotiated. Accessorial fees cover services beyond standard pickup and delivery, such as liftgate service or inside delivery. These fees can quickly add up if not closely monitored. Dimensional weight pricing adds another layer of complexity, as it considers both the weight and size of a package. Understanding these nuances is crucial for businesses to accurately forecast and manage their shipping costs. However, the lack of transparency in some pricing models means that businesses may find themselves grappling with unexpected expenses. This lack of clarity can lead to inefficiencies and financial strain, ultimately impacting the bottom line. As such, it becomes essential for businesses to insist on clear, itemized breakdowns of freight charges and to have open discussions with their 3PL partners about how these charges are determined. By sharing insights and working collaboratively, businesses can gain a better understanding of their freight charges, enabling them to make informed decisions about their shipping strategies and manage costs effectively. In the next section, we'll delve into the intricacies of hidden costs that lurk within the fine print of logistics contracts.

Hidden Costs: The Fine Print Dilemma

When it comes to working with third-party logistics providers, the devil is often in the details. The initial quote you receive may seem like a great deal, but many 3PLs have a way of burying extra costs deep within the fine print of their contracts. These hidden costs can quickly add up and catch you off guard, leading to budget overruns and frustration. It's crucial to carefully scrutinize every line of the contract to ensure you're not blindsided by unexpected charges later on. One common example of this dilemma is the handling of surcharges. While some 3PLs may advertise attractive base rates, they may conveniently fail to mention various surcharges for fuel, peak season, or special handling, which can significantly inflate your overall costs. Additionally, watch out for accessorial fees such as liftgate services, inside delivery, or reclassification charges. These seemingly minor fees can make a substantial impact on your bottom line if not accounted for upfront. The fine print dilemma also extends to terms and conditions that could put your business at risk. Pay close attention to liability clauses, insurance requirements, and indemnity provisions. Without careful review, you may unknowingly assume liabilities that should rightfully be shouldered by the 3PL. Furthermore, understanding the implications of these contractual nuances is critical to mitigating potential disputes and safeguarding your interests. Achieving transparency in pricing and contractual obligations is central to establishing a fruitful partnership with your 3PL. By taking a vigilant approach to unraveling the complexities hidden within the fine print, you can protect your business from unforeseen costs and align expectations for a successful collaboration.

Why Comparing Quotes is Like Comparing Apples to Oranges

When it comes to comparing quotes from different 3PL providers, it's easy to fall into the trap of thinking that you're making an apples-to-apples comparison. But in reality, comparing quotes can be more like comparing apples to oranges. Each 3PL has its own unique set of services, capabilities, and pricing structures, making it nearly impossible to make a direct comparison between quotes. Why? Because what might seem like a great deal on the surface could turn out to be riddled with hidden costs and limitations. As you delve deeper into the specifics of each quote, you'll quickly realize that they are not as similar as you initially thought. One provider might include certain services and charges within their base rate, while another might present these as add-ons with additional fees. It's like trying to compare the cost of a bare-bones car with a fully loaded one – they might appear to be in the same price range, but the devil is in the details. To truly compare quotes effectively, you need to understand the full scope of services included, any potential add-on fees, as well as the terms and conditions that surround the pricing. Only by gaining this comprehensive insight can you make informed decisions about which quote offers the best overall value for your specific needs. It's crucial to look beyond the surface numbers and dive deep into the specifics of each quote. By doing so, you'll be able to steer clear of unwelcome surprises down the road and ensure that you're getting exactly what you need without any unexpected costs. Remember, when it comes to comparing quotes, it's not just about the bottom line – it's about understanding the true value and ensuring that you're comparing apples to apples instead of ending up with a basket of mixed fruit.

How Discounts Can Actually Cost You More

Oftentimes, discounts can seem like a blessing. Who doesn't love saving a few bucks here and there, right? But when it comes to the complex world of logistics and 3PL pricing models, that initial discount might not be all it's cracked up to be. Let's dive into why this is the case. Imagine you're presented with a generous discount on your shipping rates from a 3PL provider. At first glance, it's an offer too good to refuse. However, what's often hidden behind that appealing discount is a web of hidden costs and fees that can quickly erode any potential savings. Here's where the devil truly lies in the details. Many 3PLs employ a tiered pricing strategy, where the more you ship, the better your discount. On the surface, this seems like a great incentive for you to increase your shipping volume to maximize your discount, but the reality is far more complicated. As your shipping volume grows, you may find yourself paying for additional services or surcharges that weren't initially factored into the discounted rate. In essence, those extra add-ons could offset any perceived savings, leaving you with a higher overall cost than if you had stuck with a more transparent, albeit modestly discounted, pricing structure. It's a classic case of the 'bargain' coming back to bite you. Moreover, some 3PLs might use these enticing discounts as a hook to lock you into long-term contracts, where exiting early incurs hefty penalties. Essentially, you're committing to a certain level of shipping with the promise of a discount, only to find that this commitment is rigid and financially punitive should your circumstances change. So, while it might initially appear that discounts are paving the way for substantial savings, the reality is often quite different. There's a delicate balance between chasing discounts and ensuring you're not lured into a financial trap. The key lies in carefully scrutinizing the fine print, understanding the true implications of those seemingly attractive discounts, and weighing them against the potential hidden costs that could ultimately undermine your bottom line.

Spot Rate Surprises: When Mutability Bites Back

We've all heard the phrase 'a deal too good to be true.' Spot rate pricing in the logistics world is a prime example of this cautionary adage. At first glance, spot rates may seem like a cost-effective solution to your freight needs, offering flexibility and potentially lower prices. However, it's essential to understand that the allure of spot rates can quickly turn into a freight management nightmare.

Spot rates are notoriously unpredictable, subject to constant fluctuations influenced by market demand, capacity constraints, and sudden shifts in fuel prices. As a shipper, relying heavily on spot rates means you're essentially at the mercy of these volatile variables. Think of it as trying to navigate turbulent seas without a reliable compass.

The seductive appeal of seemingly low spot rates might initially save you money, but as the landscape changes, so do the rates. Unforeseen spikes in spot rates due to supply chain disruptions or seasonal surges can lead to exorbitant shipping costs, eroding any initial savings and significantly impacting your bottom line. It's akin to placing a risky bet where the odds may not always be in your favor.

Furthermore, securing capacity during peak seasons or unexpected demand surges becomes increasingly challenging when reliant on spot rates. Carriers prioritize long-term commitments and contracted business, leaving shippers playing catch-up during critical periods when every shipment is time-sensitive. This results in a heightened vulnerability to delays and service inconsistencies, ultimately affecting your customer satisfaction.

Navigating the terrain of spot rates requires a delicate balance of risk evaluation and strategic planning. Understanding when to leverage spot rates and when to rely on more stable, contracted pricing models can be fundamental in mitigating the adverse impact of unpredictability on your supply chain operations. By being aware of the potential pitfalls of spot rate pricing and establishing contingency plans, you can shield your business from the adverse repercussions of abrupt rate escalations and capacity shortages. Ultimately, achieving a harmonious equilibrium between flexibility and consistency is essential for any shipper seeking to weather the storm of market volatility.

Contracts with a Twist: Penalties You Didn't Expect

Contracts with third-party logistics providers (3PLs) can contain clauses and penalties that catch businesses off guard. While the initial terms may seem favorable, it's crucial to scrutinize the fine print for potential pitfalls. One common surprise is the imposition of penalties for unforeseen circumstances such as shipment delays, inventory discrepancies, or even fluctuations in fuel prices. These unexpected costs can significantly impact your bottom line. To compound the issue, some contracts may include non-compete clauses that restrict your ability to switch to a new 3PL without incurring substantial penalties. This lack of flexibility can stifle your company's growth and competitiveness in the dynamic logistics landscape. Furthermore, certain agreements may have hidden escalation clauses, allowing the 3PL to increase pricing mid-contract without sufficient notification. This lack of transparency can lead to budgetary strain and erode trust in the partnership. It's imperative to carefully analyze the language around termination and renewal to avoid being locked into unfavorable long-term commitments. Some contracts may stipulate automatic renewals or extend notice periods, making it challenging to extricate your business from an underperforming or unsuitable 3PL. Moreover, the intricacies of billing structures and payment terms are often obscured within dense contractual jargon. Tiered pricing models, surcharges, and volume commitments can result in unforeseen expenses that were not adequately disclosed during the negotiation phase. Understanding the potential financial implications of these intricate arrangements is essential for sound decision-making. Ultimately, navigating the convoluted intricacies of 3PL contracts demands thorough due diligence. It's vital for businesses to seek legal counsel to interpret and negotiate contract terms that align with their operational needs and strategic objectives. Clear communication and mutual understanding of expectations are pivotal in fostering a collaborative partnership with a 3PL. By shedding light on these hidden clauses and potential risks, companies can safeguard themselves from unanticipated penalties and establish a more transparent and equitable contractual framework.

Transparency Talk: What Aren't They Telling You?

When it comes to selecting a 3PL provider, the issue of transparency is crucial. Many logistics companies tend to operate in a shroud of ambiguity, leaving their clients in the dark about crucial details that could impact their operations and bottom line. It's common for providers to withhold information about performance metrics, underlying costs, and potential conflicts of interest. This lack of transparency can lead to all manner of issues, from unexpected expenses to service disruptions. There are several aspects to consider when evaluating a 3PL's transparency. First, scrutinize the provider's communication regarding pricing structures, surcharges, and potential ancillary fees. It's not uncommon for providers to bury these details in fine print or omit them altogether during negotiations. Identifying these hidden costs upfront will be essential in avoiding financial surprises down the line. Next, delve into the provider's approach to data sharing and reporting. Are they willing to provide real-time visibility into your supply chain activities? Transparent reporting not only fosters trust but also facilitates proactive decision-making within your organization. Additionally, take a close look at the measures a 3PL has in place to manage potential conflicts of interest. By understanding how the provider handles relationships with carriers, warehouse facilities, and other stakeholders, you can assess the level of objectivity and fairness in their service delivery. Remember, transparency is not just an ideal; it's a necessity for a successful partnership. As you navigate the process of selecting a 3PL, don't hesitate to demand clear and comprehensive information from potential providers. Insist on transparency as a foundational principle of your collaboration, and you'll be better equipped to make sound decisions that yield long-term benefits.

Building a Pricing Blueprint You Can Trust

Pricing models in the world of third-party logistics (3PL) can often be like navigating a maze where hidden costs lurk around every corner. With this in mind, it becomes evident that building a pricing blueprint you can trust is crucial for a successful 3PL partnership. A transparent and reliable pricing plan can pave the way for a mutually beneficial relationship between you and your 3PL partner. Let's explore the fundamental elements involved in constructing a pricing blueprint that offers clarity and trust.

Firstly, understanding the full spectrum of costs involved is essential. This includes not just the obvious expenses but also the potential hidden charges that may rear their heads down the line. It's vital to work closely with your 3PL provider to gain a comprehensive insight into the pricing structure they employ and to uncover any obscured fees or contract intricacies that could impact your bottom line. Fostering open communication and clear expectations will enable both parties to align on a fair and transparent pricing arrangement.

Secondly, collaboration in refining the pricing model is key. Building a pricing blueprint should involve a collaborative effort, utilizing the expertise of both your internal team and the 3PL provider. By openly discussing and dissecting the components of the pricing structure, you can collectively identify potential areas for improvement and optimization. This collaborative approach can lead to a more tailored pricing model that accurately reflects your specific operational needs and cost considerations.

Moreover, ensuring flexibility within the pricing plan is paramount. Business landscapes are dynamic, and your pricing blueprint must have built-in adaptability to accommodate changes in demand, market conditions, and other variables. An agile pricing strategy provides the agility needed to navigate unforeseen circumstances and maintain cost-efficiency. This flexibility serves as a safety net, ensuring that your partnership with the 3PL remains resilient in the face of inevitable fluctuations.

Furthermore, establishing transparency as the cornerstone of your pricing model is essential. By proactively addressing potential grey areas or ambiguities in the pricing structure, you lay the groundwork for a trusting partnership. Being forthright about all aspects of pricing, from base rates to surcharges and beyond, cultivates a relationship based on honesty and integrity. Clear and consistent communication regarding pricing details fosters a climate of trust, underpinning the foundation of a strong and enduring collaboration.

In conclusion, crafting a pricing blueprint founded on openness, collaboration, flexibility, and transparency signifies your commitment to fostering a trustworthy and sustainable 3PL relationship. Embracing these principles empowers both parties to navigate the complexities of pricing with confidence and ensures that the partnership thrives amidst the ever-changing logistics landscape.

Logistics In The Blind Spot: Finding The Costs You Don't See

Performance Blindness

Seeing vs. Believing: The Illusion of Metrics

We often put a lot of faith in the data, assuming that it reveals the full picture. However, this blind trust can lead to a false sense of security. Traditional metrics such as on-time delivery rates or cost per unit may provide some insights, but they may not always reflect the actual performance. Take the on-time delivery rate, for example. A high percentage might look impressive on paper, but what if these deliveries are consistently late in the day, causing disruptions in downstream operations? Similarly, focusing solely on cost per unit could obscure inefficiencies hidden in the process, such as excessive handling or rerouting due to poor planning. These traditional metrics fail to capture the nuances and complexities of real-world operations. They offer a simplified, sanitized view that doesn't always align with ground reality. As we delve into the intricacies of supply chain management, it becomes clear that blindly relying on these metrics is akin to navigating through thick fog; there's a risk of missing the looming iceberg just beneath the surface. Therefore, instead of succumbing to the allure of numbers and percentages, it's crucial to adopt a more nuanced approach to performance evaluation. This includes considering qualitative factors, understanding the context behind the data, and recognizing that performance metrics are only one piece of the puzzle. By doing so, businesses can prevent falling into the trap of the illusion of metrics and gain a more comprehensive understanding of their true operational performance.

When Data Doesn't Tell the Whole Story

We live in an age where data is often hailed as the ultimate truth teller, the oracle that holds all the answers to our questions. But when it comes to understanding the intricacies of performance within the realm of logistics and supply chain management, blind faith in numbers can lead us astray. Metrics, though valuable tools in many respects, have their limitations. They provide a snapshot, a glimpse into a specific moment or aspect of operations, but they can't capture the full context or nuances that define success or failure. It's easy to get swept up in the allure of streamlined graphs and percentages, but we must remember that behind every data point lies a story—a story that may not be fully represented by the digits on the page.

Consider this scenario: A logistics manager reviews a report indicating that delivery times have improved by 15% over the past quarter. On the surface, this seems like a clear win, a testament to the efficiency of the operation. However, upon deeper investigation, it becomes apparent that this improvement came at the cost of increased shipping costs and strained relationships with carriers. Suddenly, the initial victory loses its luster, revealing a more complex narrative that the metrics failed to convey. This is not an uncommon occurrence; data can paint a deceptively rosy picture while crucial warning signs remain buried beneath the surface.

Moreover, there are realms of operational excellence that simply elude quantification. How do you measure the morale and motivation of your team, or the impact of a company-wide reorganization on individual employees? These intangibles play a significant role in the overall success of any endeavor, yet they slip through the grasp of traditional performance metrics. The limitations of data become particularly profound in times of organizational change or crisis, where the human element emerges as a critical factor in navigating through uncertainty.

The challenge, then, lies in recognizing the boundaries of what data can reveal and being vigilant about what it fails to disclose. We must cultivate a mindset that questions the stories data tells, seeking out the gaps and ambiguities that might hold the key to a deeper understanding of our operational landscape. By acknowledging the incomplete nature of our metrics, we open the door to a more holistic approach—one that integrates quantitative insights with qualitative observations, bridging the divide between cold hard numbers and the intricate tapestry of human experience within supply chain operations.

Red Flags Hidden in Plain Sight

Red flags can often be lurking just beneath the surface of seemingly smooth operations. They're the subtle signs that something might not be quite right, even if the data we rely on doesn't explicitly reveal it. These red flags are important warning signals that warrant attention and further investigation. Often, they manifest as deviations from expected patterns or performance metrics that seem inconsistent with the overall narrative. One of the challenges in recognizing these red flags is that they may not scream for attention. They could simmer quietly in the background, subtly impacting the bigger picture. In supply chain and logistics, red flags might include unexplained fluctuations in transit times, unexpected variations in order fulfillment, or irregularities in inventory management. Sometimes, they can also manifest in communication breakdowns, overlooked feedback from stakeholders, or unaddressed customer complaints. It's essential to cultivate a vigilant eye towards these potential issues, acknowledging that they could be the symptoms of deeper underlying problems. However, red flags also require cautious handling. Simply assuming the worst without a thorough understanding can lead to unnecessary panic or knee-jerk reactions.

Instead, a balanced approach involves collecting evidence, assessing the broader context, and considering multiple perspectives before drawing conclusions. Harnessing the collective wisdom of cross-functional teams and engaging in open dialogue can help identify and address these red flags effectively. Additionally, leveraging technology and analytics to detect anomalies beyond the surface-level metrics can provide valuable insights into areas that demand closer scrutiny. By shedding light on these hidden red flags, supply chain organizations can enhance their agility, resilience, and adaptability, preempting potentially disruptive events and optimizing performance. Ultimately, being attuned to red flags, hidden in plain sight, enables proactive risk management and continuous improvement, laying the groundwork for a robust and responsive supply chain ecosystem.

Getting Lost in Translation: What Does Success Really Look Like?

You might think success is obvious. It's hitting your targets, meeting your KPIs, and keeping the wheels turning smoothly. But what if that's just the surface? What if real success isn't just about numbers and metrics, but about impact and alignment with your business goals?

Consider this – you may be hitting all your predefined targets, but does it reflect the bigger picture of what really drives your business forward? Are you celebrating short-term wins, only to realize that they were distractions from your long-term vision?

When we talk about success, it's about translating the language of performance into the narrative of your business journey. It's about asking the deeper questions—does this achievement fit into our broader strategy? Is it sustainable? Are we planting seeds for future growth or just reaping quick rewards?

While data gives us valuable insights, it can also create a tunnel vision where we chase after what's measurable, ignoring the intangibles that truly define success. The translation between numbers and impact requires a keen eye, a deep understanding of the business ecosystem and a willingness to look beyond immediate gains.

And then there's the question of perspective. How do you define success? Is it solely about cost savings and operational efficiency, or does it encompass customer satisfaction, brand reputation, and long-term partnerships? As you navigate these waters, it becomes clear that success is not a one-size-fits-all concept; it morphs and adjusts with the ebbs and flows of your business landscape.

So, when assessing your performance, take a step back from the spreadsheets and charts. Look at the story they're telling beyond the numbers. Ask yourself – what does success really look like for us? And remember, the answer may not always be found in the usual places—it might be lurking in the unspoken needs of your customers, the untapped potential of your team, or the unexplored avenues of collaboration. Only then can we truly grasp the elusive essence of success and pave the way for meaningful growth and fulfillment.

The Human Factor: Are We Asking the Right Questions?

When it comes to evaluating performance, it's easy to get lost in a sea of data and metrics. However, amid all the numbers and charts, we often overlook the human factor. Are we truly asking the right questions when assessing the success of our operations? It's important to remember that behind every KPI and metric, there are real people working tirelessly to ensure that the supply chain runs smoothly. Understanding their perspective and acknowledging their challenges is crucial for accurate performance evaluation. Instead of simply focusing on whether the numbers meet the targets, we need to ask ourselves if we are supporting our team effectively. Are they equipped with the necessary resources and tools to excel? Are we providing them with opportunities for growth and development? These are the questions that shine a light on the human element of performance. Additionally, we must consider the impact of our decisions and strategies on the individuals executing them. Are we setting realistic expectations, or are we creating an environment of constant stress and burnout? By asking the right questions, we not only gain a deeper understanding of the human side of performance, but we also pave the way for holistic improvement. In doing so, we cultivate a culture of empathy and support, fostering a workforce that feels valued and empowered. It's time to shift the focus from just meeting numbers to nurturing a work environment where both the operational and human aspects thrive in harmony.

The Overlooked Signals: Looking Beyond KPIs

In the world of logistics and supply chain management, there's a tendency to rely heavily on key performance indicators (KPIs) as the barometer of success. But what if this approach is actually causing us to miss critical signals that could make or break our operations? As important as KPIs are, they only tell part of the story. Behind these numbers lie nuanced details and subtle cues that often go unnoticed, yet they hold powerful insights into the health of our logistics ecosystem. It's time to shift our focus from just hitting KPI targets to truly understanding the whys and hows behind the data. Picture this: Your on-time delivery rate meets the KPI benchmark, but further analysis reveals an upward trend in customer complaints about damaged goods upon arrival. This isn't just a statistical blip – it's a warning signal. The truth is, KPIs can sometimes provide a false sense of security, making us blind to underlying issues. We need to look beyond the numerical facades and embrace a holistic view that encompasses the real experiences of all stakeholders involved – from warehouse staff to end customers. Let's not forget that KPIs are mere reflections of the past; they inform us about what has already happened. But in a rapidly evolving supply chain landscape, we must also anticipate and prepare for what lies ahead. The overlooked signals lie in the anecdotes from frontline employees, the feedback from truck drivers, the patterns emerging from returns – these are the whispers of the supply chain telling us where attention is needed. By embracing a more expansive viewpoint, we can tap into these overlooked signals and unearth opportunities for improvement that transcend conventional metrics. It's about weaving a narrative from the mosaic of data points, one that helps us understand the intricacies and interconnections within our supply chain. Only then can we truly elevate our performance and adapt proactively to the ever-changing demands of the market.

Blame It on the Algorithms: Tech Shortcomings and How They Shape Perception

In today's digital age, algorithms play a pivotal role in shaping our understanding of performance metrics within the realm of logistics and supply chain management. These complex, often opaque formulas are designed to crunch vast amounts of data and generate insights that aid decision-making. However, reliance solely on these algorithms can lead to a series of tech shortcomings that significantly impact how we perceive the overall performance of 3PL operations. One key issue is the potential bias encoded within algorithms, stemming from the data input or the inherent design. This bias has the potential to skew the perceptions of success or failure, leading to a distorted view of operational efficiency.

Moreover, algorithms are inherently limited by the data they are provided. In the logistics and supply chain domain, with its myriad variables and interconnected processes, it's easy for algorithmic systems to miss crucial contextual information or fail to account for nuanced factors that may influence overall performance. These limitations can greatly affect the accuracy and reliability of the insights derived from them. Furthermore, the rapid evolution of technology means that algorithms may struggle to keep up with the changing demands and dynamics of 3PL operations. As a result, they might be ill-equipped to offer a real-time, comprehensive view of performance.

The black box nature of algorithms presents another hurdle — the lack of transparency regarding the inner workings of these systems. This opacity can create a sense of distrust and apprehension among stakeholders, as they struggle to comprehend the basis upon which critical decisions are being made. When algorithms operate behind a veil of secrecy, it becomes difficult to pinpoint where and how their outputs are influenced, leading to a disconnect between the generated metrics and the actual ground reality. This can sow doubt and hinder informed decision-making, posing a significant challenge in accurately assessing the true performance of 3PL operations.

Navigating through these tech shortcomings demands a deeper comprehension of the limitations of algorithms and a proactive approach in mitigating their influence on perception. By understanding the biases, limitations, and opacity associated with algorithms, stakeholders can adopt a more discerning approach to interpreting their outputs. Moreover, supplementing algorithmic insights with human expertise and intuition fills the gaps left by tech. Through open dialogue and collaboration, organizations can work towards refining these algorithms and ensuring that they provide a more accurate depiction of performance. Only then can the overarching aim of leveraging technology to gain actionable insights be fully realized, empowering stakeholders to make more informed decisions that drive the success of 3PL operations.

Transparency Hurdles: Why It's Hard to See Clearly

In the complex world of 3PL relationships, achieving full transparency can feel like chasing a mirage in the desert. Many factors contribute to the ongoing struggle to gain a clear, unobstructed view of performance and operations. One significant hurdle is the inherent complexity of the supply chain itself. With multiple stakeholders, interconnected processes, and a myriad of data points, achieving transparency demands a cohesive, well-integrated approach. Furthermore, proprietary systems and disparate technology platforms often create silos of information, making it challenging to access comprehensive, real-time insights. Additionally, the reluctance or inability of some 3PL partners to share certain aspects of their operations can further obscure the landscape. This lack of openness may stem from concerns about revealing vulnerabilities or from ingrained cultural practices that prioritize secrecy over collaboration. Furthermore, the industry's historical emphasis on glossy, high-level metrics can inadvertently mask underlying issues, promoting an illusion of transparency while concealing critical details. The prevalence of standardized reports and dashboards can sometimes present a veneer of clarity, but they often fail to capture the nuanced complexities and anomalies within the supply chain. Moreover, misaligned incentives and objectives sometimes lead to selective disclosure, further muddying the waters. Finally, the human element cannot be overlooked. Even with access to data, interpreting and understanding the implications behind the numbers requires a deep understanding of both the business and the partner's operational intricacies. Misinterpretations, biases, and differing interpretations can cloud the view, hindering true transparency. Confronting these hurdles demands a proactive, collaborative effort rooted in trust and mutual understanding. Only by acknowledging the challenges and addressing them head-on can stakeholders pave the way toward clear, actionable transparency.

Lessons from the Field: Real-Life Stories of Performance Wake-Up Calls

You know, sometimes the best way to understand the impact of performance blindness is through real-life stories. Let's face it, we all love a good story, especially when it comes with a powerful lesson. In our journey through the logistics world, we've come across some eye-opening experiences that have reshaped the way we view performance in the supply chain. One story that stands out is about a company that relied heavily on KPIs and metrics to gauge the performance of their 3PL partner. Everything seemed fine on paper, but behind the scenes, there were consistent delays, communication breakdowns, and inventory discrepancies that weren't captured by the numbers. It wasn't until a major client raised concerns about late deliveries and inaccurate stock levels that the reality hit home. Suddenly, the illusion created by the seemingly positive metrics crumbled, and the need for a clearer, more holistic view became glaringly obvious. Another tale comes from a small e-commerce startup that believed technology would solve all their logistical challenges. They invested in state-of-the-art tracking systems and automated processes, yet they couldn't figure out why customer complaints were skyrocketing. The realization struck when an employee who personally handled customer inquiries noticed a pattern of shipping errors that the automated system had missed. These tales illustrate the crucial point that numbers alone don't always reveal the full truth. Embracing the human experience and understanding the real operational dynamics are key elements in gaining a comprehensive view of logistics performance. It's the pivotal turning point that prompts companies to look beyond the surface and seek the hidden cues that define true success. By sharing these narratives, we hope to underscore the vital importance of acknowledging and learning from the unexpected stories that lurk beneath the data-driven facade. Only by recognizing and rectifying these blind spots can companies truly elevate their understanding of logistics performance and steer toward visionary strategies that transcend mere numbers.

Bridging the Gap: Tools for Gaining a Clearer View

To overcome performance blindness and gain a clearer view in the logistics industry, it's crucial to leverage the right tools and strategies. One of the most effective tools is investing in advanced data analytics and visualization software. These tools can help businesses dissect complex data sets, identify patterns, and uncover insights that might otherwise remain hidden. By visualizing key performance indicators (KPIs) and metrics in intuitive dashboards and reports, decision-makers can quickly grasp the dynamics at play and make informed decisions. Furthermore, implementing proactive monitoring and alert systems can provide real-time visibility into critical operational aspects, enabling timely interventions when performance falters.

Beyond technology, fostering a culture of transparency and open communication is essential for bridging the gap in understanding performance. This involves breaking down silos between different departments and stakeholders, as well as promoting a shared understanding of organizational objectives and key performance drivers. By creating a collaborative environment where feedback flows freely, businesses can address blind spots and gain alignment on what truly matters for success. Additionally, conducting regular performance reviews and debriefs can engage the team in reflective discussions that lead to actionable improvements.

In the quest for a clearer view, it's also vital to embrace a holistic approach that goes beyond traditional metrics. Incorporating qualitative feedback from customers, employees, and partners offers valuable perspectives that quantitative data alone may not capture. Voice of the customer programs, employee engagement surveys, and supplier relationship assessments are just some avenues for gathering qualitative insights that contribute to a comprehensive understanding of performance. Moreover, leveraging benchmarking and industry best practices can provide context for interpreting performance data, uncovering areas for enhancement, and setting realistic targets.

Finally, as businesses strive to bridge the gap in performance visibility, they must consider the role of education and skill development. Providing training on data literacy, analytical tools, and interpretation of performance metrics equips employees with the competence to navigate through data complexities and draw meaningful conclusions. Empowering the workforce to distill information and translate it into actionable initiatives strengthens the organization's ability to bridge the gap and achieve better outcomes. In summary, a combination of advanced tools, transparent culture, holistic feedback sources, and continuous learning is instrumental in gaining a clearer view and overcoming performance blindness in the logistics realm.

Logistics In The Blind Spot: Finding The Costs You Don't See

Building Transparency into Your 3PL Relationship

The Trust Factor: Why Transparency Matters

Trust is the bedrock of any successful relationship, and the partnership with your 3PL provider is no exception. When it comes to logistics operations, cultivating an environment of openness and honesty is crucial. This section delves into the critical role that trust plays in building transparency within your 3PL relationship. By fostering a culture of trust, both parties can openly communicate their needs, concerns, and expectations, creating a solid foundation for collaboration. Without trust, there's a risk of misinterpretation, misunderstandings, and ultimately, operational friction. It's essential for both you and your 3PL provider to acknowledge the significance of mutual understanding. With transparency as the cornerstone, trust acts as the glue that binds all aspects of the partnership together. A transparent approach promotes accountability and integrity, enabling seamless information sharing and decision-making. In an environment where trust thrives, you can expect improved problem-solving, streamlined processes, and enhanced efficiency. Ultimately, by placing trust at the forefront of your relationship, you pave the way for a productive and harmonious collaboration with your 3PL provider.

Knowing What You Need: Setting the Stage for Open Communication

Setting the stage for open communication in your 3PL relationship starts with a clear understanding of what you truly need. It's about identifying not just what you want from your 3PL partner, but also what you absolutely need to drive your business forward. This means taking a deep dive into your operations, goals, and pain points. Ask yourself and your team tough questions. What inefficiencies are holding you back? What critical information is missing? What are the non-negotiables for your supply chain? Once you've pinpointed these needs, it becomes much easier to map out how transparent communication can address them. Open communication isn't just about sharing everything; it's about sharing the right things at the right time. It means creating clarity around what data, metrics, and insights are essential for both parties. By knowing what you need, you're setting the groundwork for a proactive, communicative partnership where expectations are clear and success is more achievable. When you clearly communicate your needs, you're also inviting your 3PL partner to do the same. This reciprocity fosters trust and collaboration, laying a solid foundation for the transparent, successful 3PL relationship you're aiming for.

Making Expectations Crystal Clear

When it comes to building transparency into your 3PL relationship, one of the most crucial aspects is ensuring that your expectations are crystal clear from the get-go. This not only involves outlining your specific needs and requirements but also delving into the finer details that can often be overlooked. As you embark on this journey of clarity, it's imperative to communicate openly and honestly with your 3PL partner. Discussing your expectations in depth lays the foundation for a solid and transparent relationship. Clearly defining your expectations goes beyond simply stating what you want; it entails articulating the why behind each requirement. By providing your 3PL partner with insight into your underlying motivations, you enable them to align their operations with your broader objectives. This level of understanding enhances the chances of a successful partnership. Moreover, it fosters a sense of collaboration and mutual respect, setting the stage for effective communication throughout the entire engagement. Communicating expectations clearly not only relates to the results or outcomes you envision but also encompasses the process and timeline expectations. It's essential to outline the specific deliverables, quality standards, and performance metrics that will define success. Additionally, discussing timelines and deadlines provides your 3PL partner with a clear understanding of when certain milestones need to be achieved. This contributes to a more efficient and synchronized operation. Transparency in expectations also entails addressing any potential challenges or obstacles that may arise. Being upfront about these possibilities helps to manage expectations and establish contingency plans. Openly acknowledging the hurdles that could surface demonstrates a proactive approach and reinforces the mindset of transparency within the relationship. Furthermore, this proactive stance prompts proactive problem-solving, positioning both parties to address challenges collaboratively. Embracing this open dialogue around potential roadblocks nurtures an environment of trust and resilience. By making expectations crystal clear, you lay the groundwork for a robust, transparent 3PL relationship that is built on a shared understanding of objectives, processes, and potential hurdles.

Information Flow: How to Keep it Constant and Consistent

Information is the lifeblood of any successful 3PL relationship. Without constant and consistent information flow, misunderstandings can arise, trust can erode, and performance can suffer. So, how do you keep the tap flowing? First and foremost, establish regular communication channels. This could be weekly check-ins, monthly reports, or a shared digital platform for real-time updates. The key is to set a rhythm that suits both parties and stick to it. Next, ensure that the information exchanged is clear, relevant, and actionable. Avoid flooding your partner with unnecessary data, but don't skimp on vital details either. In addition, embrace transparency in reporting. Don't just share the good news; be upfront about challenges and setbacks. Being open about the hurdles allows for collaborative problem-solving and builds a stronger, more resilient partnership. It's also essential to clarify information ownership. Clearly define who is responsible for collecting, analyzing, and disseminating data to avoid confusion or duplication of effort. Furthermore, technology can be a game-changer in maintaining a constant flow of information. Consider investing in tools that streamline data sharing and provide visibility into key metrics. Finally, strive for consistency. Establish and adhere to standardized processes for information exchange to minimize errors and ensure everyone is working from the same playbook. By prioritizing a steady, reliable flow of information, you'll lay a solid foundation for trust, collaboration, and ultimately, success in your 3PL relationship.

Cracking Open the Books: Creating Financial Openness

Transparency in finances is like shedding light on the heartbeat of your 3PL relationship. After all, trust shouldn't stop at operational transparency; it should extend into financial matters as well. In any partnership, especially one as complex as a 3PL relationship, money talks – and so should you. Creating financial openness starts with a fundamental shift in mindset. It's about more than just revealing numbers; it's about fostering an environment of trust and collaboration.

To achieve true financial openness, both parties must be willing to lay their cards on the table – figuratively speaking, of course. This means being upfront about costs, pricing structures, and potential areas for cost savings. One key aspect of this openness is ensuring that all parties fully understand the billing process, fee structures, and any potential additional charges. By creating a clear line of sight into the financial intricacies of the partnership, you set the stage for open and honest communication that transcends mere transactional discussions.

Another crucial element of financial openness is the ability to explore and address any disparities or incongruities in financial data. This requires a commitment to regular, thorough financial reviews, where both parties have the opportunity to dissect and discuss the numbers. These conversations aren't just about scrutinizing figures; they lay the foundation for identifying areas of improvement and innovation. Whether it's uncovering hidden inefficiencies or recognizing opportunities for shared cost reductions, these discussions are instrumental in nurturing a sense of shared responsibility and investment in mutual success.

Furthermore, creating financial openness involves embracing real-time reporting and insights. Instead of relying on delayed reports or periodic updates, the aim is to access financial data as it happens. This promotes agility and informed decision-making, allowing both sides to respond promptly to any fluctuations or trends. Moreover, real-time insights foster a dynamic approach to problem-solving and strategy development, enabling both parties to make proactive adjustments and capitalize on emerging opportunities.

Overall, building financial openness within your 3PL relationship isn't just about fiscal data; it's about weaving a tapestry of transparency, trust, and mutual respect. By cracking open the books and embracing financial openness, you pave the way for a partnership grounded in shared goals, collaborative problem-solving, and collective growth.

Real-Time Updates: Not Just a Fantasy

In the complex web of logistics and supply chain management, real-time updates often seem like an elusive dream. But guess what? They don't have to be! In today's fast-paced world, the ability to access immediate, accurate information is not just a luxury—it's a necessity. Real-time updates provide you with a valuable window into the heart of your 3PL operations. Imagine being able to track your shipments, monitor inventory levels, and receive instant notifications about any unforeseen events or delays. This level of transparency empowers you to make informed decisions and respond promptly to changing situations. To achieve this, leveraging advanced tracking technologies and robust communication systems is crucial. By integrating these tools into your 3PL relationship, you can transform real-time updates from fantasy into reality. Whether it's through RFID tags, GPS tracking, or sophisticated software platforms, staying connected to your cargo as it moves through the supply chain becomes increasingly feasible. Real-time updates don't just benefit you—they also enhance the collaboration between you and your 3PL partner. When you both have access to the same instantaneous data, trust deepens, problems are identified and solved faster, and misunderstandings are minimized. It's a win-win for everyone involved. However, incorporating real-time updates isn't without its challenges. From navigating data security concerns to ensuring seamless integration with existing systems, there are hurdles to overcome. Yet, with strategic planning and open communication, these obstacles can be successfully managed. The importance of investing in this aspect of transparency cannot be overstated. As technology continues to advance, the gap between fantasy and reality shrinks. Embracing real-time updates as a fundamental component of your 3PL relationship will position you at the forefront of a more efficient and responsive supply chain landscape.

Feedback Loops: Keeping the Conversation Alive

In the world of logistics and supply chain management, communication is key. Building transparency into your 3PL relationship isn't just about sharing information—it's about fostering an ongoing dialogue that keeps both parties in sync and on track. This is where feedback loops come into play. A feedback loop is a mechanism through which the outputs of a system are circled back as inputs, with the goal of improving the system's performance. When it comes to your 3PL partnership, establishing effective feedback loops is essential for maintaining transparency and driving continuous improvement. One of the fundamental elements of a successful feedback loop is creating an environment where all stakeholders feel empowered to share their insights, concerns, and suggestions. Whether it's through regular meetings, online platforms, or open-door policies, providing multiple channels for feedback ensures that valuable information doesn't get lost in transit. Beyond simply receiving input, it's equally important to demonstrate a commitment to acting upon that feedback. This might involve implementing process changes, adjusting service levels, or addressing specific pain points raised by your 3PL partner. By actively responding to feedback, you not only show that you value the input provided but also signal that transparency is a two-way street. Additionally, transparency flourishes when there is clarity around how feedback is incorporated into decision-making processes. Defining clear procedures for reviewing and acting on feedback helps to maintain trust and accountability within the partnership. Moreover, technology plays a vital role in enabling robust feedback loops. From sophisticated data analytics tools to user-friendly survey platforms, leveraging technology can streamline the process of collecting, analyzing, and disseminating feedback. Real-time reporting and dashboards can offer visibility into performance metrics, allowing both parties to identify trends and address issues proactively. Implementing technology-driven feedback mechanisms can transform the exchange of information from sporadic events into a continuous, real-time flow. Ultimately, cultivating effective feedback loops fosters a culture of openness and collaboration, strengthening the foundation of your 3PL relationship. By acknowledging the importance of feedback, responding thoughtfully, and harnessing technology to facilitate communication, you ensure that the conversation remains lively, constructive, and conducive to mutual growth.

Tools of the Trade: The Role of Technology in Transparency

In today's fast-paced world, the role of technology in creating transparency within 3PL relationships cannot be overstated. The right technological tools can revolutionize the way information is shared, accessed, and utilized between your business and your 3PL partner. Through advanced software solutions, communication platforms, and data management systems, technology plays a pivotal role in fostering openness and clarity.

One vital aspect where technology makes a substantial difference is in real-time visibility. With state-of-the-art tracking systems and IoT-enabled devices, both you and your 3PL partner can monitor every step of the supply chain journey. This heightened visibility not only enhances trust and accountability but also allows for proactive issue resolution and performance optimization. Furthermore, these technological advancements enable you to obtain granular insights into inventory levels, shipment statuses, and order fulfilment, empowering you to make informed decisions that strengthen your supply chain operations.

The integration of cloud-based platforms also serves as an invaluable tool in promoting transparency. By centralizing data storage and accessibility, cloud technologies facilitate seamless information sharing and collaboration. This fosters a culture of transparency as it eliminates silos and promotes a unified understanding of critical data. Moreover, by harnessing analytics tools embedded within these platforms, you can gain comprehensive dashboards and reports that shed light on key performance metrics, allowing for intelligent strategic planning and continuous improvement initiatives.

Another essential component of technology in transparency revolves around communication channels. Interactive portals and real-time messaging systems ensure that communication flows freely and consistently. Through these mediums, you and your 3PL partner can swiftly address issues, share updates, and align on goals, fostering a relationship built upon honesty and cooperation. Additionally, the use of automated notifications and alerts keeps all stakeholders informed about relevant developments, guaranteeing that no crucial information slips through the cracks.

When exploring the role of technology in transparency, the emphasis should also be placed on data security and privacy. Robust cybersecurity measures are crucial to maintaining the integrity and confidentiality of the shared information. By adopting encryption protocols, access controls, and regular security audits, technology acts as a safeguard against unauthorized access or breaches, ensuring that sensitive data remains secure and protected.

Ultimately, technology serves as the conduit through which transparency thrives. By investing in innovative tech solutions, businesses can establish an environment of openness, trust, and collaboration with their 3PL partners. It's not just about leveraging the latest gadgets; it's about using technology as a catalyst for building stronger, more transparent relationships that drive mutual success.

Challenges and Solutions: Navigating the Speed Bumps

Facing challenges is inevitable, especially when striving for transparency in your 3PL relationship. One of the prominent speed bumps companies encounter is the resistance to change. Implementing a transparent system often requires a shift in mindset and operations, which can be met with reluctance or skepticism from both internal and external stakeholders. Additionally, legacy systems and processes may pose significant obstacles, creating inertia against adopting new, more transparent practices.

In navigating these challenges, it's crucial to firstly acknowledge and address the sources of resistance. Open, honest communication about the benefits of transparency and the rationale behind the changes is essential to gaining buy-in from all parties involved. This involves not just sharing the 'what' and 'how' of transparency, but also articulating the 'why' in a compelling manner that resonates with everyone impacted.

Another hurdle is the fear of vulnerability. Some may perceive transparency as a risk, fearing that airing out operational intricacies could invite criticism or scrutiny. A key solution to this challenge lies in fostering a culture of trust and psychological safety within the organization. Encouraging open dialogue, celebrating learning opportunities from mistakes, and promoting a growth mindset can help mitigate these apprehensions and demonstrate the value of transparency as a catalyst for improvement.

Moreover, technological barriers can impede the seamless flow of information essential for transparency. Outdated IT infrastructure, disparate data sources, and inadequate integration capabilities often hinder the real-time visibility and accessibility required for transparency. Overcoming these hurdles involves investing in modern technologies and robust integration solutions that can bridge the informational silos, ensuring synchronized data exchange and actionable insights.

Furthermore, cultural misalignments within your 3PL partner's organization can also pose a substantial challenge. Differences in organizational values, communication styles, or even conflicting priorities may hinder the establishment of a shared transparent framework. Addressing these challenges entails cultivating a mutual understanding of each other's cultures, fostering empathy, and establishing common ground through collaborative efforts toward transparency.

Ultimately, surmounting these challenges necessitates a comprehensive approach that integrates people, processes, and technology. Embracing transparency isn't merely an organizational change; rather, it's a cultural transformation that demands perseverance, empathetic leadership, and proactive problem-solving. By recognizing and proactively addressing these challenges, you pave the way for not only navigating the current speed bumps but also steering toward a future defined by openness, trust, and mutual success.

A Transparent Future: What's on the Horizon

As we look to the future, the landscape of 3PL relationships is evolving. The concept of transparency is no longer a mere buzzword but a non-negotiable aspect of successful partnerships. In the coming years, technology will continue to play a pivotal role in fostering transparency. We can expect to see the emergence of advanced tracking and reporting tools that provide real-time visibility into every stage of the supply chain. From predictive analytics to blockchain technology, the tools at our disposal will empower us to make data-driven decisions with unprecedented precision and foresight. Moreover, these innovations will not only enhance transparency but also streamline processes, improve efficiency, and ultimately reduce costs. Alongside technological advancements, the future will demand a mindset shift toward proactive transparency. This means actively sharing information, insights, and even vulnerabilities before they escalate into issues. Organizations that can foster this culture of openness will undoubtedly gain a strategic advantage in an increasingly competitive market. Furthermore, as the industry continues to grapple with complex global challenges such as geopolitical uncertainties and sustainability concerns, transparency will be key to maintaining resilience and adaptability. It will pave the way for collaborative problem-solving, innovation, and ethical business practices. As we continue to innovate and adapt, the concept of transparency may extend beyond the traditional boundaries of the supply chain. We could see increased emphasis on transparency throughout the entire value network, from sourcing raw materials to the end consumer. Companies that can establish end-to-end visibility and accountability will build greater trust and loyalty among consumers and partners alike. Ultimately, the transparent future holds immense potential for reshaping the dynamics of 3PL relationships, driving value creation, and fostering a new era of collaboration and trust.

Logistics In The Blind Spot: Finding The Costs You Don't See

Choosing the Right 3PL Partner

Kicking Things Off: Know What You Need

Before diving into the search for a 3PL partner, it's crucial to fully grasp your own logistical needs and priorities. This isn't just about what you think you need; it's about what you really need. Consider the specific requirements of your business operations, the volume and frequency of shipments, the nature of your products, and any seasonal variations. An honest assessment of your current logistical challenges can bring valuable clarity. Are there recurring bottlenecks or areas where you constantly hit snags? Are there gaps in service that have held your operations back? What are the pain points screaming out for resolution? It's also essential to forecast future needs — growth ambitions, potential shifts in market demand, and expansion plans need to be factored in. Understanding your own logistics landscape will not only help you identify the type of assistance required from a 3PL partner but also enable you to ask the right questions when evaluating potential candidates. Additionally, knowing what you don't need is equally significant. Identifying areas where you already excel and where external intervention might not be necessary will save both time and resources. Your tailored 3PL solution should aim to complement and reinforce your existing strengths while addressing existing pain points. Remember, the perfect match is one that aligns with your goals and values, and resonates with the heartbeat of your business. By investing time in self-assessment, you set a strong foundation for the collaborative journey ahead.

Peeking Under the Hood: Researching Potential Partners

Researching potential partners for your 3PL relationship is like embarking on a detective mission. You're not just looking for basic information, but you're also trying to uncover the hidden details and red flags that may not be immediately obvious. First things first, start with a thorough online search. Look into their company website, social media presence, and any articles or reviews about them. This will give you an initial sense of their reputation and the types of services they offer. Dig deeper into their track record. Explore case studies, customer testimonials, and industry accolades if available. This can provide valuable insights into their past performance and reliability. Make sure to also check for any warning signs such as legal issues, financial instability, or operational hiccups. Don't hesitate to reach out to industry peers for recommendations and feedback. Attend trade shows and networking events to connect with potential partners in person. This allows you to gauge their professionalism, interpersonal skills, and overall company culture. When seeking out potential partners, consider the size and scope of their operations. Are they equipped to handle your specific needs, both now and in the future? Is their network of facilities strategically located to optimize your supply chain? Pay attention to the technology and systems they utilize. Do they align with your own, or would integration be a struggle? Look for evidence of innovation and continuous improvement. The right partner should be adaptable and forward-thinking, constantly seeking better ways to serve their clients. Lastly, don't underestimate the importance of values alignment. Seek out partners who share similar beliefs and priorities, particularly in areas like sustainability, ethical business practices, and community engagement. Remember, this research phase sets the foundation for a successful long-term partnership. Take your time, ask the tough questions, and trust your instincts.

The Heart-to-Heart: Initial Conversations and Rapport Building

When it comes to choosing the right 3PL partner, remember that initial conversations and rapport building are pivotal in setting the tone for your future collaboration. This phase is all about establishing a genuine connection, understanding each other's goals, and assessing the potential for a long-term partnership. As you engage in these discussions, focus on creating an environment of openness and transparency. You want to ensure that both parties feel comfortable sharing their expectations, concerns, and vision for the partnership. This is where the human element truly shines through in the decision-making process. Emphasize the importance of active listening, as it allows both sides to truly understand each other's needs and challenges. Encourage open dialogue and ask relevant questions to gain deeper insights into their approach, values, and problem-solving strategies. Remember, this isn't just about evaluating their capabilities; it's also about gauging the chemistry and synergy between your teams.

While it's essential to cover logistical aspects like service offerings, technology solutions, and industry expertise, don't overlook the cultural fit. Assessing whether your organizational values align with those of the potential partner is crucial. Consider how they handle communication, conflict resolution, and adaptability to change. Look for signs of proactiveness and a willingness to go the extra mile to support your unique business requirements. Beyond the professional conversations, take the time to get to know the individuals representing the 3PL provider. Building trust and rapport with key personnel can lay a strong foundation for future collaborations and problem-solving scenarios. By fostering a shared sense of purpose and mutual respect from the outset, you pave the way for a relationship built on trust and understanding.

Remember, establishing solid rapport at this stage sets the stage for a successful and fruitful partnership. It's not just about ticking off checkboxes; it's about finding a partner who shares your vision, understands your challenges, and is committed to helping you overcome them. Approach these initial conversations with authenticity, curiosity, and a genuine desire to build a lasting and mutually beneficial alliance.

Seeing Beyond the Sales Pitch: Evaluating Real Capabilities

When it comes to choosing the right third-party logistics (3PL) partner, a key step is seeing beyond the sales pitch and evaluating the real capabilities of potential providers. It's easy to get swept away by compelling presentations and promises, but it's crucial to dig deeper to ensure that a 3PL can truly deliver on its commitments. This section will guide you through the process of evaluating a 3PL's real capabilities.

It starts with a mindset shift - from being passive recipients of information to active investigators. Engage in thorough conversations to understand the depth of experience and innovation the provider brings to the table. Ask incisive questions that reveal their problem-solving approach, adaptability, and commitment to continuous improvement.

Next, move beyond surface-level assurances and seek tangible evidence of performance. Request case studies, client testimonials, or even site visits to witness operations firsthand. Scrutinize not just what they say, but what they show. Don't be swayed by flashy presentations; instead, look for substance and consistency.

Simultaneously, evaluate the scalability and flexibility of the 3PL's operations. Are they equipped to handle both the current needs of your business and potential future growth? Delve into their technology infrastructure, operational processes, and workforce capabilities to gauge their capacity to adapt to evolving requirements.

A critical aspect often overlooked is the alignment of cultural values. Assess whether the provider's ethos resonates with your company's ethos. A harmonious cultural fit can significantly impact the success of the partnership, fostering better collaboration and understanding.

Moreover, scrutinize the clarity and transparency in communication. Open and honest dialogue is fundamental to a successful relationship. How responsive and forthcoming are they in addressing your concerns? The way they communicate reflects their professionalism and commitment to building a sustainable partnership.

Ultimately, evaluating real capabilities involves a comprehensive assessment that goes beyond mere assurances. It's about understanding the provider's track record, approach to challenges and change, and their willingness to collaborate as a true extension of your business. This critical evaluation sets the foundation for a mutually beneficial and enduring

3PL partnership.

Crunching Numbers and Going Beyond: Understanding the Pricing

When it comes to choosing the right 3PL partner, understanding the pricing models is crucial. It's not just about the numbers; it's about uncovering the true value behind them. As you delve into the pricing structures offered by potential partners, it's essential to go beyond the surface. Asking for detailed breakdowns and explanations of all costs involved can shed light on what's truly being offered. Dive into the fine print and don't shy away from asking tough questions. What seems like a good deal on the surface might not hold up under scrutiny. Look for transparency in the pricing, and if something seems too good to be true, there's a chance it might be. It's also vital to consider the long-term implications of the pricing models. A partner offering lower upfront costs might end up being more expensive in the long run due to hidden fees or limited capabilities. On the flip side, a higher initial investment might translate to better quality service and long-term cost savings. Consider the scalability of the pricing as well. Will the partner be able to accommodate your business's growth without significantly increasing costs? Additionally, factor in the value-added services that may not be immediately apparent in the pricing structure. Some partners may offer added benefits such as advanced reporting, proactive communication, or innovative technology solutions that can significantly impact your operations and bottom line. As you crunch the numbers, keep an eye out for opportunities to negotiate terms that align with your long-term goals. Remember, the goal is not just to find the most affordable option, but rather the partner that offers the best overall value and fit for your business. By understanding the pricing models and going beyond the surface, you'll be better equipped to make an informed decision that will benefit your business in the long run.

Tech Talk: Ensuring Compatibility and Innovation

As we delve into the technological aspect of choosing a 3PL partner, it's crucial to ensure compatibility between your systems and theirs. This involves looking beyond basic integrations and understanding how their technology can seamlessly integrate with yours. Compatibility also extends to future innovations - you don't want to be stuck with a partner whose technology becomes obsolete in a few years. Ask about their approach to innovation and how they stay ahead of the curve. Are they open to adopting new technologies that could benefit your operations? It's also vital to discuss data security and privacy measures. With the increasing threat of cyber attacks, you need to be certain that your business's sensitive information will be safeguarded. In an era where data breaches make headlines, this is non-negotiable. Additionally, inquire about their tech support and troubleshooting processes. When something goes awry, you want to know that they have a responsive team ready to assist. Beyond these considerations, think about scalability. As your business grows, will their technology grow with you? Discuss your future projections and understand how their systems can adjust to accommodate increasing demands. The last thing you want is to outgrow your 3PL partner's technology and find yourself in need of a replacement sooner than anticipated. Remember, technology is not just a tool, but an enabler of efficiency, visibility, and agility. Choosing a partner with the right technology can propel your supply chain to new heights of competitiveness and responsiveness. These discussions may seem technical, but they are pivotal in shaping a partnership that will drive success for years to come.

Flexibility, Please: Discussing Adaptability and Scalability

When it comes to choosing the right 3PL partner, adaptability and scalability are crucial factors to consider. In our ever-evolving business landscape, the ability to adjust and grow alongside your company is paramount. Let's dive into the discussion on flexibility with a magnifying glass, shall we? Flexibility in a 3PL partner means having the agility to respond to changing market demands, adjusting to seasonal fluctuations, and accommodating unexpected shifts in your supply chain. When you sit down at the negotiation table, it's imperative to outline various scenarios and assess how the potential partner would handle each one. Furthermore, evaluating their track record of adapting to industry changes provides valuable insight into their capabilities. But let's not stop there—scalability is equally vital. As your business expands, your 3PL partner must have the resources and infrastructure to grow with you. Delve into discussions about their capacity to handle increased volumes, expanded geographic reach, or additional service offerings. It's not just about where they are now, but where they can be in the future. Asking for case studies or success stories of how they've seamlessly scaled up operations for other clients can offer a glimpse into their potential to support your growth. An open dialogue regarding your long-term vision and how the 3PL partner aligns with it is essential. Additionally, ensure that their technology and systems can accommodate your future needs without significant disruptions. By addressing adaptability and scalability head-on, you'll pave the way for a partnership that can weather the storms and scale to new heights with your business.

Cultural Fit: Aligning Values and Work Ethics

When it comes to choosing the right 3PL partner, compatibility in terms of culture, values, and work ethics is often overlooked but holds significant importance. The collaboration between your company and a 3PL partner needs to be based on shared values and a similar approach towards work. It's crucial that both parties align in terms of their organizational culture, as this will determine how well they can work together effectively. Understanding each other's values and work ethics is not only about ensuring alignment but also forging a strong and enduring partnership.

Cultural fit goes beyond mere likability or personal rapport – it delves into how business is conducted, decision-making processes, and the level of transparency and communication expected. Therefore, when evaluating potential 3PL partners, it becomes imperative to assess if their organizational culture aligns with yours. Do they prioritize integrity, innovation, and continuous improvement? How do they handle challenges and conflicts? Are they open to feedback and committed to fostering a collaborative environment? These are just a few questions that need careful consideration.

Moreover, cultural fit directly influences the day-to-day interactions and operational dynamics between your company and the 3PL partner. If the underlying values clash, it can lead to miscommunication, friction, and ultimately hinder the achievement of shared objectives. On the contrary, when there's cultural harmony, it paves the way for streamlined processes, mutual trust, and a seamless workflow. The shared work ethics contribute to a conducive environment for problem-solving, idea exchange, and maintaining high standards of service.

Remember, cultural misalignment can impact not only the immediate business operations but also the long-term viability of the partnership. Establishing a strong cultural fit acts as a solid foundation for building a lasting and prosperous relationship with your 3PL provider. It signifies a commitment to shared goals, mutual respect, and a willingness to evolve together. Thus, while weighing the pros and cons of different 3PL partners, pay close attention to whether their cultural values and ethics resonate with your own, as this can have far-reaching implications for the success of your collaboration.

Reference Check with a Twist: Getting Honest Feedback

As you narrow down your options for a 3PL partner, reference checks can provide valuable insights to help inform your decision. However, traditional reference checks may not always reveal the full picture. To get a deeper understanding, consider taking a more nuanced approach.

First, identify key contacts within the companies that have worked with your potential 3PL partners. Rather than relying solely on the references provided by the 3PL, utilize your network to connect with others who have experience working with them. This outside perspective can offer a more comprehensive view of the partner's strengths and limitations.

When reaching out for feedback, aim to gather specific anecdotes and examples that highlight the partner's performance in crucial situations. Ask about challenges they faced and how the 3PL responded. Understanding their problem-solving approach and adaptability in real scenarios can give you a clearer picture of what it would be like to work with them.

In addition to inquiring about operational aspects, delve into the interpersonal dynamics. How does the 3PL communicate with their clients? Are they responsive and transparent in their interactions? Learning about these softer skills is just as important as understanding their technical capabilities.

Moreover, seek input from references beyond the immediate point of contact. Engage with individuals across various levels of the organization, from warehouse staff to upper management. This broad spectrum of perspectives can uncover trends and patterns that might otherwise go unnoticed.

Finally, don't shy away from asking tough questions. While it's natural to focus on the positive attributes of potential partners, it's equally crucial to unearth any pain points or areas for improvement. By approaching the reference check with an open mind and a discerning eye, you can gain a more balanced understanding of what to expect.

Ultimately, while data and statistics provide valuable insights, the human touch and personal experiences shared through reference checks can offer nuanced wisdom that shouldn't be overlooked when making such a pivotal decision.

Final Decision: Trust Your Instincts and Data

The moment of truth has arrived. After meticulously researching and evaluating potential 3PL partners, it's time to make that final decision. This is where you need to trust both your instincts and the data you've gathered throughout the selection process. While data provides valuable insights and measurable metrics, your instincts play a crucial role in assessing the intangible aspects of a partnership.

When it comes to choosing the right 3PL partner, it's essential to strike a balance between rational analysis and gut feelings. The data might steer you towards a seemingly perfect fit based on performance indicators, cost-efficiency, and technological prowess. However, your instincts can offer a unique perspective on how well the partnership aligns with your company's culture, values, and long-term vision.

Take a step back and reflect on the larger picture. Trust your instincts when it comes to assessing the compatibility of personalities and organizational ideologies. Can you envision a seamless collaboration? Do you feel a sense of trust and mutual respect during interactions with the potential partner? These subtle cues play a significant role in determining the success of your future collaboration.

On the other hand, rely on the wealth of data you've collected to validate and support your intuition. Analyze the metrics, feedback, and references gathered from multiple sources. Look for patterns and discrepancies, and use this objective information to corroborate or challenge your initial impressions. Combining instinctual reactions with empirical evidence creates a holistic approach to making the final decision.

Furthermore, seek validation from key stakeholders within your organization. Encourage open discussions and gather diverse opinions. Their insights can provide valuable layers of perspective that might complement or challenge your own assessments. Remember to engage in constructive dialogue rather than seeking confirmation bias; the goal is to leverage collective wisdom to ensure a well-rounded decision-making process.

Ultimately, understand that no partnership is entirely risk-free. While data and instincts guide your decision, there's still an element of uncertainty inherent in any business relationship. Embrace this uncertainty with cautious optimism, knowing that thorough preparation and a balance of rationality and intuition can pave the way for a successful 3PL partnership. Trust in your ability to analyze, assess, and decide, equipped with both informed judgment and intuitive wisdom.

Logistics In The Blind Spot: Finding The Costs You Don't See

Measuring What Matters

Kicking Things Off: Why Measurement Matters

Understanding the importance of metrics when evaluating 3PL performance is key to ensuring long-term success and efficiency. As businesses strive for operational excellence, it becomes imperative to define and measure success effectively. What are we really after when we talk about measuring what matters? It's about aligning our goals with tangible outcomes and ensuring that we have a clear understanding of what success looks like. This involves going beyond surface-level metrics and diving deep into the core objectives of our logistics operations. By setting clear measurements, we can create a roadmap that guides us toward achieving our desired outcomes. When it comes to 3PL performance, these measurements provide us with valuable insights into the efficiency, reliability, and overall effectiveness of our logistics partners. We need to kick things off by recognizing that measurement matters, not just for tracking progress, but for driving real, meaningful improvements. Metrics give us the power to identify areas for enhancement, optimize processes, and ultimately deliver superior customer experiences. They act as a compass, helping us navigate through the complexities of the supply chain landscape. Furthermore, robust measurement practices enable us to hold our 3PL partners accountable and foster a culture of continuous improvement. Without a clear focus on measurement, our efforts run the risk of becoming aimless and ineffective. By embracing the importance of metrics, we lay the foundation for proactive decision-making, resource allocation, and strategic alignment. Ultimately, this leads to enhanced competitiveness and sustainability in an ever-evolving market environment.

Defining Success: What Are We Really After?

Success isn't just a finish line we race toward; it's also a destination we must first map out. When it comes to measuring the effectiveness of your 3PL partnership, success can take many forms, each as unique as the business it serves. Defining what success looks like for your company is crucial before diving into measurement metrics. This isn't about finding a one-size-fits-all solution; instead, it's about identifying the specific goals and objectives that align with your overarching business strategy. Ask yourself: What are the core drivers of our organization? Is it rapid fulfillment times, cost efficiency, customer satisfaction, or a combination of these and more? By pinpointing these key factors, you lay the groundwork for what success truly means. In this modern age, it's not always just about hitting performance quotas; it's about embodying excellence at every touchpoint of the supply chain. To define success, consider both quantitative and qualitative aspects. Sure, numbers matter, but so does the experience your customers receive and the impact on your brand reputation. Perhaps success means reducing transit times by 20%, decreasing error rates in order processing, or enhancing overall customer satisfaction. Maybe it involves achieving sustainability targets or fostering innovation and adaptability within your supply chain. Remember that success is multidimensional and requires a holistic approach to measure effectively. This chapter will guide you through the process of articulating what success means for your business and how to translate those aspirations into tangible, measurable goals.

The Metrics That Matter Most: Don't Drown In Data

Understanding the metrics that truly matter is like finding the needle in the haystack. In the world of 3PL, data can be overwhelming – volumes of numbers, statistics, and reports that seem endless. It's easy to feel lost, juggling KPIs and performance indicators without a clear sense of direction. But amidst this sea of information, there are key metrics that carry the most weight; they are the true pulse of your operations. One such critical metric is on-time delivery. This cutthroat, competitive marketplace heavily relies on timely delivery as a cornerstone of customer satisfaction. It's not just about reaching the deadline; it's also about consistency and predictability in meeting those deadlines. Another pivotal metric is order accuracy - getting the right products to the right people at the right time. With the complexity of modern supply chains, a slip in order accuracy can lead to disastrous consequences. Keeping a vigilant eye on inventory accuracy is non-negotiable. Inventory holding costs and stockouts due to inaccurate data can wreak havoc on your bottom line. Furthermore, the all-important cost per order must be accurately weighed. This metric encapsulates the holistic cost of every transaction, from processing to shipment. While minimizing costs is crucial, compromising service quality in pursuit of cost efficiency would be self-defeating. Additionally, employee productivity is an often overlooked yet immensely significant metric. The efficiency and effectiveness of your workforce directly impact your operational success or failure. Assessing and improving productivity involves understanding how well resources are being utilized and identifying areas for optimization. Lastly, the customer satisfaction score serves as a crucial compass. This metric goes beyond the numbers, reflecting the overall customer experience. From communication and responsiveness to issue resolution and relationship building, it encompasses the entirety of the customer journey. By focusing on these key metrics, you can steer clear of drowning in irrelevant data and instead navigate with purpose toward operational excellence. Recognizing what truly matters allows you to develop actionable insights and make informed decisions that drive your business forward.

Getting Real: Setting Achievable Benchmarks

Setting achievable benchmarks is essential for measuring the success of your 3PL operations. It's not just about setting lofty goals and hoping for the best—it's about creating realistic targets that push your business forward while also being attainable. By setting benchmarks that are too high, you risk demoralizing your team and creating a culture of unattainable expectations. On the other hand, setting benchmarks that are too low can result in complacency and a lack of motivation to strive for improvement. So, how do you strike the right balance? Start by analyzing historical data and performance trends within your organization. This will provide valuable insights into what is realistically achievable based on past performance. Consider industry standards and best practices to understand what targets are considered reasonable and attainable for businesses similar to yours. It's also important to involve relevant stakeholders when setting benchmarks. By including input from various departments and key personnel, you can ensure that the targets set align with the overall goals and capabilities of the organization. Moreover, involving employees in the benchmark-setting process can foster a sense of ownership and commitment to meeting those targets. When establishing benchmarks, it's crucial to consider the specific characteristics and challenges of your 3PL operations. Factors such as the complexity of your supply chain, the nature of your products, and the unique demands of your customers should all be taken into account. These factors will influence the feasibility of certain benchmarks and help tailor them to your specific circumstances. Additionally, keep in mind that benchmarks should be adaptable. As your business evolves and market conditions change, it's important to review and adjust your benchmarks accordingly. Flexibility is key to ensuring that your benchmarks remain relevant and motivating over time. Finally, communicate clearly and transparently about the benchmarks you set. Make sure that everyone involved understands the rationale behind each benchmark and the metrics used to measure progress. This clarity will help align efforts across different teams and departments towards achieving common goals. With carefully crafted and achievable benchmarks, you can effectively track and improve the performance of your 3PL operations, steering your business towards sustained success.

Customer Satisfaction: It's Not Just a Number

We often talk about customer satisfaction as if it's a single, tangible metric. Sure, you might see a score or a rating next to the words 'customer satisfaction,' but what does that really tell you? Numbers can only convey so much. Real customer satisfaction is so much more than a figure on a spreadsheet or a star rating on a survey. It's about understanding your customers on a deeper level, and knowing that their needs are being not just met, but exceeded. When we talk about customer satisfaction in the context of your 3PL relationship, it goes beyond just asking your clients to rate their experience from 1 to 10. It's about actively engaging with them to understand their pain points, their successes, and their vision for the future. Are they truly satisfied with the service provided? Do they feel valued and heard? Are their unique needs being understood and addressed? These are the questions that need to be answered. Customer satisfaction is about building and nurturing relationships. It's about recognizing that each client is a unique entity with their own expectations and requirements. You need to have systems in place to collect feedback, but also the willingness to act on that feedback. Your goal should be not just to meet the needs of your customers, but to anticipate them. Happy customers are your best ambassadors, and dissatisfied ones can spread negativity faster than wildfire. Your 3PL provider should share this perspective – understanding that the success of your business depends on the satisfaction of your customers. Together, you and your 3PL provider can work towards delivering an experience that goes beyond just fulfilling an order, but leaves a lasting impression. Ultimately, customer satisfaction is not just a metric, it's a mindset, a culture, and a commitment to excellence.

Time is Money: Evaluating Speed and Efficiency

In the world of logistics, time isn't just a concept - it's money. Every delay, every inefficiency, every moment wasted has a direct impact on your bottom line. But evaluating speed and efficiency goes beyond just clocking in and out. It's about understanding the intricate dance of processes, people, and technology that make up your supply chain.

When we talk about speed, we're not just talking about how quickly your products move from point A to point B. We're talking about the entire journey - from order processing to delivery. It's about streamlining every step, eliminating bottlenecks, and ensuring that your goods are moving at the optimal pace throughout the entire process.

But speed without efficiency is like a race car running on fumes. You might be moving fast, but you're burning resources along the way. Efficiency is about doing more with less - optimizing your resources, minimizing waste, and maximizing output. It's about finding ways to streamline operations, automate repetitive tasks, and constantly fine-tune your processes to achieve peak performance.

Evaluating speed and efficiency requires a deep dive into your operations. It means analyzing every touchpoint, every handoff, and every interaction within your supply chain. It's about looking for opportunities to reduce lead times, consolidate shipments, and eliminate unnecessary steps. It's also about leveraging technology to track and measure every aspect of your operations - from warehouse movements to transportation routes.

But it's not just about moving faster and doing more. It's about doing the right things faster. It's about understanding the critical paths in your operations and focusing your efforts on the areas that will yield the greatest impact. It's about identifying where speed and efficiency can drive value for your customers, improve your bottom line, and give you a competitive edge in the market.

So, when we talk about evaluating speed and efficiency, we're looking beyond the surface. We're diving deep into the inner workings of your supply chain, uncovering opportunities for improvement, and harnessing the power of time to propel your business forward.

Cost Control: Keeping Tabs on the Dollars

When it comes to managing a third-party logistics (3PL) program, cost control is one of the most critical aspects. The key to effective cost control lies in the ability to monitor and manage expenses at every stage of the logistics and supply chain process. By keeping a watchful eye on the dollars, companies can identify potential areas of waste, streamline operations, and ultimately improve their bottom line.

The first step in maintaining cost control is establishing clear and transparent pricing structures with your 3PL partner. This means going beyond just the basic rates and understanding the various surcharges, accessorial fees, and other related costs that could impact your overall expenses. By gaining a clear understanding of these charges, you can effectively negotiate and ensure that you are not being hit with unexpected costs.

Another crucial element of cost control is leveraging technology to track and analyze expenditures. Advanced data analytics and reporting tools can provide valuable insights into where money is being spent, allowing for informed decision-making. Additionally, implementing cost-saving technologies such as automated inventory management systems or real-time shipment tracking can contribute to efficient cost control strategies.

Moreover, fostering a culture of cost consciousness within your organization is vital. Educating employees about the impact of their decisions on overall cost and encouraging them to seek more economical solutions can lead to significant savings. Furthermore, establishing clear accountability and responsibility for cost management across all levels of the company can help ensure that everyone is aligned with the overarching cost control objectives.

It's also essential to regularly review and benchmark your costs against industry standards and best practices. This can provide valuable context and highlight areas that may require improvement. By staying aware of market trends, regulatory changes, and emerging technologies, companies can adapt their cost control strategies to remain competitive and efficient.

Lastly, effective cost control is not just about cutting expenses; it's also about increasing value. Understanding that cost reduction should not compromise service quality is crucial. Striking the right balance between cost and service excellence is what sets successful companies apart. Ultimately, by keeping tabs on the dollars, businesses can optimize their

3PL programs, drive operational efficiencies, and deliver greater value to their customers.

Quality over Quantity: The True Measure of Value

When it comes to the world of logistics and supply chain management, the age-old adage 'quality over quantity' holds more truth than ever before. In today's hyperconnected, fast-paced business environment, it's easy to become fixated on sheer volume and speed, often at the expense of quality. However, the wise leaders in this space understand that true value lies not just in the numbers, but in the precision, reliability, and consistency that underpin every aspect of their operations. Quality is the cornerstone of enduring success. But what exactly does quality mean in the context of logistics? It's about ensuring that every link in the chain, from sourcing and production to transportation and delivery, meets or exceeds established standards. This entails a relentless commitment to accuracy, safety, and adherence to regulations, as well as a keen eye for innovation and improvement. It's a mindset that rejects complacency and demands excellence at every turn. Traditionally, the pursuit of quality has been associated with higher costs, as superior inputs and processes naturally come at a premium. Yet, in the long run, investing in quality pays off manifold. Whether it's fewer errors, reduced waste, enhanced customer satisfaction, or improved brand reputation, the benefits are substantial and sustainable. To truly appreciate the significance of quality, one must also recognize its direct impact on the bottom line. In an industry where every dollar counts, the notion of 'value over cost' can make all the difference. Embracing a quality-first approach empowers companies to differentiate themselves in a crowded marketplace, attract discerning customers, and strengthen relationships with partners and suppliers. After all, in today's discerning market, it's the organizations that consistently deliver the highest levels of quality that stand out amidst the noise. Of course, achieving and maintaining superior quality is no simple task. It demands a holistic perspective, proactive problem-solving, and a perpetual quest for enhancement. From leveraging cutting-edge technology and automation to implementing stringent quality control measures and fostering a culture of continuous improvement, success hinges on a multifaceted strategy. With quality serving as the lodestar, businesses can lay the groundwork for enduring success, resilience, and competitive advantage. The intangible yet unmistakable essence of quality permeates every facet of the supply chain, culminating in a finely woven tapestry of credibility, dependability, and trust. By embracing 'quality over quantity' as a guiding principle, logistics and supply chain leaders not only elevate their operations but also enhance the overall industry landscape. Within this framework, value isn't just a concept—it's a quantifiable outcome achieved through unwavering commitment to quality.

Feedback Loop: Turning Insight into Action

In the world of third-party logistics, the ability to turn insights into action is crucial. Without a solid feedback loop in place, all the data and analytics can quickly become meaningless. It's not enough to simply collect information on key metrics and performance indicators – it's what you do with that information that truly matters. This chapter is all about understanding the power of feedback and using it to drive meaningful change within your logistics operations.

Feedback is a two-way street, and it should be an ongoing process rather than a one-time event. It's not just about receiving input from your 3PL provider or other stakeholders; it's also about providing them with feedback on their performance and the impact it has on your business. Open and transparent communication is vital for the success of any feedback loop. It's important to create an environment where all parties feel comfortable sharing their perspectives, concerns, and suggestions without fear of reprisal.

Effective feedback should be specific and actionable. Vague or generalized feedback doesn't provide much value when it comes to making improvements. By providing clear, specific feedback, you can help your 3PL partner understand exactly what areas need attention and what changes are required to drive better outcomes. This targeted approach enables them to take meaningful action based on the insights they receive from your feedback.

Another key aspect of the feedback loop is the ability to track progress and measure the impact of any changes that are implemented as a result of the feedback. This requires establishing clear benchmarks and KPIs (key performance indicators) that can help you gauge the effectiveness of the actions taken. Regular review and analysis of this data allow you to refine strategies, address any emerging issues, and capitalize on opportunities for improvement.

Moreover, a successful feedback loop extends beyond just addressing immediate concerns or challenges – it also involves forward-thinking and proactive discussions. By leveraging the insights gained through feedback, you can identify trends, anticipate future needs, and make strategic decisions that align with your overall business objectives. This forward-looking approach positions your logistics operations to stay agile and responsive in a fast-evolving business landscape.

Ultimately, the feedback loop serves as a catalyst for continuous improvement and innovation. It's not just about reacting to issues as they arise; it's about constantly seeking ways to enhance performance, add value, and foster a collaborative partnership. A well-functioning feedback loop empowers both you and your 3PL provider to adapt, grow, and thrive in an ever-changing marketplace.

Bringing It All Together: A Balanced Scorecard

You've gathered data, analyzed trends, and identified areas for improvement - now what?

It's time to bring it all together with a balanced scorecard. This comprehensive framework allows you to evaluate your 3PL performance across multiple dimensions, helping you gain a holistic view of your logistics operations.

The balanced scorecard goes beyond traditional financial metrics to include non-financial measures that are critical for long-term success. By incorporating key performance indicators (KPIs) related to customer satisfaction, operational efficiency, and quality control, the balanced scorecard provides a more complete picture of your 3PL provider's performance.

When designing your balanced scorecard, consider the perspectives that matter most to your business - typically, these include financial, customer, internal processes, and learning/growth. Each perspective should have its own set of KPIs that align with your overarching goals and objectives. For example, under the customer perspective, you might track on-time delivery rates, order accuracy, and responsiveness to customer inquiries.

It's important to strike a balance between leading and lagging indicators on your scorecard. Lagging indicators, such as cost per order or inventory turnover, reflect past performance, while leading indicators, like employee training hours or process cycle time, offer insights into future potential. By incorporating both types of indicators, you can gauge not only what has happened, but also what is likely to happen in the future.

In addition, the balanced scorecard encourages continuous improvement by fostering a culture of accountability and transparency. Regularly reviewing and discussing the scorecard results with your 3PL partner fosters collaboration and ensures that everyone remains aligned with the same overarching objectives. It also provides an opportunity to celebrate successes and identify areas for further development.

Ultimately, the balanced scorecard serves as a powerful tool for aligning your 3PL provider's performance with your strategic goals, driving continuous improvement, and fostering a mutually beneficial partnership. By carefully selecting the right KPIs and regularly monitoring and adapting your scorecard, you can ensure that your logistics operations are not just meeting, but exceeding expectations. As you integrate the balanced scorecard into your management practices, you'll be better equipped to make informed decisions and drive meaningful change within your supply chain.

Logistics In The Blind Spot: Finding The Costs You Don't See

From Blind Spot to Strategic Advantage

Unpacking the Hidden Opportunities

When it comes to unlocking potential, it's crucial to shift our focus from the obvious to the overlooked. Unpacking the hidden opportunities entails delving into the uncharted territories of our operations and processes. Often, innovative solutions and avenues for growth lie dormant in these unnoticed areas. By scrutinizing each step of the supply chain, we can reveal untapped potential and uncover new opportunities for improvement and expansion. Furthermore, by embracing a mindset geared toward exploration and curiosity, we can develop a heightened awareness of the concealed prospects within our organization. It's akin to discovering a treasure trove that was previously hidden in plain sight. The journey of unpacking hidden opportunities is not just about identifying them; it involves harnessing their potential to drive transformative change. Whether it's streamlining logistics, optimizing inventory management, or reimagining customer experiences, the process of uncovering hidden opportunities demands both creativity and intentionality. It invites us to think beyond conventional boundaries and reimagine the status quo. In doing so, we unveil novel approaches that resonate with the demands of today's dynamic market landscape. Embracing the pursuit of uncovering hidden opportunities creates an environment ripe for innovation and growth, positioning us at the forefront of progress and evolution. As we venture into unexplored horizons and dissect the intricacies of our operations, we unearth the foundations for pioneering solutions that propel our organization forward. Ultimately, unpacking the hidden opportunities isn't just an exercise in discovery; it is an assertion of our commitment to perpetual advancement and a testament to our adaptability in the face of change.

Changing Your Lens: Seeing Potential

Your perspective is your reality. How you view challenges, obstacles, and opportunities can significantly impact your ability to adapt, evolve, and thrive in an ever-changing business landscape. In the realm of logistics and supply chain management, this notion holds tremendous weight. Too often, companies view their weaknesses solely as liabilities, overlooking the untapped potential waiting to be unlocked. To transform your organization's blind spots into strategic advantages, it's imperative to undergo a fundamental shift in perspective. This begins with changing the lens through which you perceive your operational shortcomings. Rather than perceiving weaknesses as inherent deficits, start by reframing them as unexplored sources of strength. Consider how these areas of vulnerability can be leveraged to propel your business forward. By embracing this mindset, you'll uncover a wealth of resources, capabilities, and innovative solutions that were previously obscured. Embracing change can be daunting, but viewing challenges as fertile ground for growth unleashes a wave of ingenuity and creativity within your team. As you begin to sketch a new portrait of your organizational landscape, identify the dormant potential hiding within your blind spots. By cultivating a culture that celebrates innovation and resilience, you empower your workforce to adopt a dynamic, solution-oriented mindset. This shift not only revolutionizes your approach to problem-solving but also catalyzes a ripple effect of positive change throughout your entire operation. Through the lens of potential, every obstacle becomes an opportunity, every weakness a reservoir of untapped strength. Step into this transformative mindset and watch as your blind spots metamorphose into pillars of strategic advantage.

Turning Weakness into Strength

In the world of logistics and supply chain management, weaknesses are a part of the game. They come in various forms - from process inefficiencies to technology gaps, and from performance blindness to pricing models that hide more than they reveal. Acknowledging these weaknesses is the first step towards transformation. It's about recognizing that weaknesses hold the potential for growth and improvement. Instead of viewing them as roadblocks, we need to see them as opportunities to turn the tide. One key aspect of turning weakness into strength is identifying the root causes behind these weaknesses. Whether it's a lack of visibility into key metrics or a disconnect between different stages of the supply chain, understanding the underlying issues is crucial. This understanding paves the way for targeted solutions that can address these weaknesses head-on. Moreover, turning weakness into strength involves a mindset shift. It's about fostering a culture of continuous improvement and innovation within the organization. This means encouraging open communication, sharing insights, and empowering employees to contribute ideas for overcoming weaknesses. Collaboration is another vital ingredient in this journey. By forging strong partnerships with 3PL providers who understand your unique challenges, you can leverage their expertise to shore up your weaknesses and build on your strengths. Furthermore, learning from past mistakes and experiences can be instrumental in the process of transformation. It's okay to stumble, as long as we use those moments as stepping stones towards progress. Embracing an agile approach allows us to adapt and evolve, transforming our weaknesses into adaptive strengths. At the heart of this transformation lies the recognition that weaknesses are not immutable barriers, but rather opportunities for growth and advancement. By embracing these challenges, we have the chance to emerge stronger, more resilient, and better positioned for success in the competitive landscape of modern logistics and supply chain management.

Learning to See More Clearly

In the journey towards turning weakness into strength and bridging the gap with innovation, there lies a crucial phase of learning to see more clearly. This phase is about shedding light on the aspects that were previously obscured by blind spots and gaining insights that lead to informed decisions and strategic moves. Through introspection and analysis, you can start to peel back the layers of complexity and truly understand the dynamics at play within your organization and its relationship with 3PL providers.

Seeing more clearly involves leveraging data and analytics to uncover patterns, trends, and performance indicators that were once hidden from view. By harnessing the power of technology and integrating advanced tracking systems, you can gain real-time visibility into your supply chain operations, inventory management, and overall logistics performance. This newfound clarity allows you to identify inefficiencies, anticipate potential disruptions, and make proactive adjustments that align with your strategic objectives.

Moreover, learning to see more clearly also entails cultivating a culture of transparency and open communication within your organization and with your 3PL partners. Establishing clear channels for feedback, reporting, and collaboration enables stakeholders to share valuable inputs, raise concerns, and work together towards mutually beneficial solutions. Embracing transparency nurtures trust and encourages a collective effort to address challenges head-on, thereby fostering continuous improvement and innovation.

Furthermore, gaining clearer visibility requires embracing adaptability and agility in response to evolving market dynamics and customer demands. By staying attuned to industry trends, customer behavior, and macroeconomic shifts, you can anticipate changes and position your organization for success. This proactive approach empowers you to capitalize on emerging opportunities and mitigate potential risks, thus creating a competitive advantage in the marketplace.

As you embark on the journey of learning to see more clearly, you must also be prepared to challenge conventional thinking and explore unconventional solutions. Embracing a mindset of curiosity, creativity, and exploration opens doors to new perspectives and breakthrough ideas. By breaking free from traditional norms and venturing into uncharted territory, you can discover innovative approaches that propel your organization forward and set it apart from the competition.

Ultimately, the process of learning to see more clearly is a transformative endeavor that reshapes the way you perceive challenges, opportunities, and the entire landscape of 3PL relationships. It equips you with the acumen to navigate complexities, anticipate changes, and leverage insights for strategic decision-making, ultimately driving your organization towards achieving a sustainable and resilient supply chain ecosystem.

Bridging the Gap with Innovation

In today's rapidly evolving business landscape, bridging the gap between potential blind spots and strategic advantage requires a keen focus on innovation. Innovation is not just about groundbreaking technologies or disruptive ideas—it's about harnessing creativity and ingenuity to address challenges and drive growth. As you navigate the complexities of third-party logistics (3PL) and supply chain management, embracing innovation becomes paramount. It's no longer enough to simply identify blind spots; you must actively seek out innovative solutions to mitigate risks and leverage untapped opportunities. One way to bridge this gap is by fostering a culture of continuous improvement and forward thinking within your organization. Encouraging your teams to think outside the box and explore new approaches can lead to transformative breakthroughs. Furthermore, embracing technological advancements is essential in bridging these gaps. Whether it's implementing advanced analytics to gain greater visibility across your supply chain or leveraging automation to streamline processes, technology plays a pivotal role in driving innovation. Collaborating with industry experts, thought leaders, and even cross-functional teams within your own organization can also fuel innovation. By pooling diverse perspectives and expertise, you can uncover novel strategies and best practices that propel your operations from blind spots to strategic advantage. As you embark on this journey of innovation, it's crucial to remain agile and adaptable. The ability to pivot and respond swiftly to market changes and customer demands is a hallmark of successful innovators. This agility allows you to continuously refine your strategies and stay ahead of the curve. Finally, data-driven insights serve as a cornerstone for innovation. Leveraging the power of data analytics and predictive modeling empowers you to make informed decisions and anticipate future trends. By tapping into valuable insights, you can proactively identify blind spots and capitalize on emerging opportunities. Ultimately, bridging the gap with innovation is about embracing change, staying curious, and daring to challenge the status quo. As you integrate innovation into the fabric of your 3PL and supply chain operations, you'll not only transform potential blind spots into strategic advantages but also position your organization as a trailblazer in the industry.

Collaborating for Success

In the journey from identifying blind spots to leveraging them as strategic advantages, the role of collaboration cannot be overstated. Rather than working in silos, successful organizations understand the power of collaborative efforts that bring together diverse perspectives, skill sets, and experiences. Collaborating for success goes beyond mere cooperation; it's about harnessing the collective intelligence and creativity of your team to tackle challenges and seize opportunities.

Effective collaboration involves building a culture of trust and transparency where individuals feel empowered to contribute, share ideas, and take calculated risks. It means breaking down barriers that hinder open communication and cross-functional collaboration. When everyone in the organization feels valued and heard, they become more invested in the outcomes and are willing to go the extra mile to achieve shared goals.

Furthermore, successful collaboration demands a mindset shift from competition to cooperation. It's about recognizing that everyone brings unique strengths to the table and that by working together, those strengths can complement and elevate one another. Foster an environment where individuals are encouraged to embrace diversity of thought and approach problem-solving collectively. By doing so, you not only tap into a wealth of innovative ideas but also create a sense of belonging and unity within the team.

Moreover, collaborating for success extends beyond internal teamwork. It entails forging strategic partnerships with external stakeholders, including suppliers, customers, and industry peers. By aligning goals and resources, organizations can leverage each other's expertise and networks to create mutually beneficial outcomes. These partnerships can lead to shared innovation, expanded market reach, and increased resilience in the face of industry disruptions.

Lastly, technology plays a pivotal role in facilitating collaboration in today's interconnected world. From cloud-based platforms for seamless information sharing to project management tools that foster virtual collaboration, the right technology infrastructure can empower teams to work together irrespective of geographical boundaries.

In essence, mastering the art of collaborating for success is about fostering an environment that encourages open communication, embraces diversity, cultivates trust, and leverages technology to harness the collective potential of a team and its strategic partners.

Creating a Culture of Agility

In today's rapidly changing business landscape, agility has become a key factor for success. A culture of agility enables organizations to respond quickly to market shifts, customer needs, and technological advancements. But what does it mean to create a culture of agility within your organization? It goes beyond just being able to move fast; it's about fostering a mindset that embraces change, experimentation, and continuous improvement. Agility is not just a buzzword; it's a way of thinking and working that can give your business a competitive edge. Creating a culture of agility starts with leadership. Leaders need to advocate for and model agile behaviors, such as flexibility, adaptability, and a willingness to take calculated risks. This sets the tone for the entire organization and empowers employees to embrace change and innovation. Open communication and collaboration are also essential components of an agile culture. Teams need to be empowered to make decisions, experiment with new ideas, and learn from both successes and failures. This requires a shift away from traditional hierarchical structures towards more dynamic, cross-functional teams that can quickly mobilize to address challenges and seize opportunities. Another critical aspect of building agility is a focus on learning and development. Employees should be encouraged to continually enhance their skills and knowledge, staying abreast of industry trends and best practices. This not only keeps your workforce competitive but also fosters a culture of innovation and adaptability. Embracing technology and digital transformation is vital in creating a culture of agility. Leveraging data-driven insights, automation, and streamlined processes allows companies to pivot swiftly and make informed decisions. It's about harnessing the power of technology to optimize operations and stay ahead of the curve. Lastly, celebrating and recognizing agile behaviors and outcomes reinforces a culture of agility. When employees see that their agility and innovation efforts are valued and rewarded, they're more likely to continue exhibiting these traits. Incorporating agility into performance metrics and recognizing agile achievements contributes to a culture that champions responsiveness and forward thinking. Ultimately, creating a culture of agility is an ongoing journey that requires commitment, adaptability, and a willingness to challenge the status quo. By nurturing an environment where change is embraced and continuous improvement is championed, organizations can transform their blind spots into strategic advantages.

Tapping Into Insights and Data

In today's competitive landscape, having the ability to tap into insights and data is indispensable for businesses seeking sustainable growth. In this digital era, data has become the new currency, and the organizations that harness its power are the ones that thrive. For 3PL providers and their clients, leveraging data provides a strategic advantage in optimizing supply chain operations and enhancing decision-making processes.

Accurate, real-time insights derived from data analytics enable stakeholders to gain a comprehensive understanding of their supply chain performance. From inventory management and demand forecasting to transportation routing and warehouse optimization, data-driven insights pave the way for smarter, more efficient operations. By tapping into this wealth of information, businesses can identify patterns, trends, and potential bottlenecks, enabling proactive interventions to streamline processes and drive continuous improvement.

Moreover, insights derived from data allow 3PL providers to offer value-added services to their clients. With enhanced visibility into key metrics such as on-time delivery rates, order accuracy, and inventory turnover, 3PLs can proactively collaborate with their clients to identify areas for improvement and implement tailored solutions. This collaborative approach fosters stronger partnerships built on mutual success and a shared commitment to ongoing optimization.

However, simply accumulating data isn't enough; the real value lies in deriving meaningful insights from it. This necessitates the use of advanced analytics tools and technologies that can process extensive datasets and extract actionable intelligence. From predictive analytics to machine learning algorithms, the capabilities provided by modern data analytics empower businesses to make informed, data-driven decisions that directly impact their bottom line.

Embracing a culture that prioritizes data-driven decision-making equips organizations with the agility needed to adapt to market shifts and evolving customer demands. Through the compilation and analysis of diverse datasets, companies can uncover hidden opportunities, uncover operational inefficiencies, and pivot strategies accordingly. By integrating insights and data into their organizational DNA, businesses establish a foundation for sustained success and resilience in the face of industry dynamics.

Ultimately, tapping into insights and data isn't merely a technological pursuit; it's a mindset that permeates an organization's ethos. It's about embracing the transformative potential of data and leveraging it to not only stay ahead in the game but also pioneer new standards of excellence in supply chain management. As we delve deeper into this topic, we'll explore how forward-thinking businesses leverage data to drive innovation, fuel growth, and set the stage for a future where insights pave the way forward.

Staying Ahead in the Game

In today's fast-paced and ever-changing business environment, staying ahead in the game is crucial for success. With the increasing complexity of supply chains and the growing demand for efficiency and innovation, companies need to continuously adapt and evolve to maintain their competitive edge. Staying ahead means embracing change, being proactive, and constantly seeking new ways to improve and optimize operations. One key aspect of staying ahead in the game is the ability to anticipate market trends and customer needs before they become mainstream. By tapping into insights and data, companies can gain a deeper understanding of market dynamics and consumer behavior, allowing them to pivot and adjust their strategies in advance. This foresight not only helps them stay ahead but also positions them as industry leaders. Another vital factor in staying ahead is fostering a culture of agility and adaptability within the organization. This involves empowering employees to think innovatively, take calculated risks, and rapidly respond to market shifts. Companies that encourage a nimble mindset are better equipped to navigate unpredictable challenges and capitalize on emerging opportunities. Furthermore, staying ahead requires a commitment to continuous improvement and learning. Embracing new technologies, refining processes, and investing in upskilling employees are all critical components of maintaining a competitive advantage. By staying abreast of industry developments and proactively integrating cutting-edge solutions, companies can position themselves at the forefront of innovation. It's also about collaborating with partners and stakeholders to leverage collective expertise and resources. Collaboration enables companies to exchange knowledge, share best practices, and co-create innovative solutions, propelling them to the forefront of industry advancement. Ultimately, staying ahead in the game is about not just reacting to change but driving it. It involves challenging the status quo, reimagining possibilities, and charting new paths to success. Companies that embrace this mindset position themselves as market leaders, setting the pace for others to follow.

Your Strategic Advantage Blueprint

So, you've worked through the challenges and opportunities, navigated the complexities, and now stands on the brink of transforming your supply chain operations from a potential blind spot into a genuine strategic advantage. But how do you ensure that this transformation isn't just a fleeting moment of success, but a sustained accomplishment? That's where the 'Strategic Advantage Blueprint' comes into play. This blueprint is not merely a static plan; it's a dynamic, evolving framework designed to keep your organization ahead in the game for the long haul.

The first crucial aspect of this blueprint involves a comprehensive evaluation of your current strengths and weaknesses. By conducting a thorough assessment, you can identify areas where you already hold an advantage, as well as pinpoint opportunities for improvement. This evaluation forms the bedrock upon which your strategic advantage will be built.

Next, your blueprint should outline specific goals and timelines. What are the milestones you aim to achieve, and over what period? These goals should be attuned to both short-term wins and long-term strategic positioning. They will act as guides, keeping you focused and accountable as you progress along your transformation journey.

Central to the blueprint is the cultivation of a culture that promotes agility and innovation. This involves empowering your team to think creatively, encouraging risk-taking, and fostering an environment where change is embraced rather than feared. A forward-thinking approach will enable you to adapt rapidly to market shifts and technological advancements, ensuring that your strategic advantage remains relevant in an ever-evolving landscape.

Another pivotal element of the blueprint lies in leveraging insights and data. Your organization must have robust mechanisms in place to capture, analyze, and act upon real-time information. By harnessing the power of data analytics and predictive technologies, you can make informed, proactive decisions that keep you steps ahead of the competition.

Finally, sustaining this strategic advantage requires ongoing collaboration with key partners and stakeholders. By forging strong alliances built on transparency and mutual benefit, you can tap into new resources, knowledge, and opportunities that amplify your competitive edge.

Remember, your 'Strategic Advantage Blueprint' isn't a one-time endeavor – it's a living, breathing strategy that demands continual refinement and adaptation to stay ahead in the game. Embrace the dynamism, uphold an unwavering commitment to excellence, and watch as your organization transforms a once-hidden blind spot into an enduring source of strength and success.

www.ingramcontent.com/pod-product-compliance
Lightning Source LLC
Chambersburg PA
CBHW031448210526
45464CB00005B/2365